LEADERS
MADE
HERE

Other books by the author:

Chess Not Checkers

The Heart of Leadership

The Secret of Teams

The Secret with Ken Blanchard

Great Leaders Grow with Ken Blanchard

Related Field Guides:

The Secret with Randy Gravitt

Chess Not Checkers with Randy Gravitt

The Heart of Leadership

The Secret of Teams

BUILDING A LEADERSHIP CULTURE

LEADERS MADE HERE

MARK MILLER

Bestselling Author of *Chess Not Checkers*
and *The Heart of Leadership*

BK

Berrett–Koehler Publishers, Inc.
a BK Business book

Berrett-Koehler Publishers, Inc.
1333 Broadway, Suite 1000
Oakland, CA 94612-1921
Tel: (510) 817-2277   Fax: (510) 817-2278   www.bkconnection.com

Ordering Information

Quantity sales. Special discounts are available on quantity purchases by corporations, associations, and others. For details, contact the "Special Sales Department" at the Berrett-Koehler address above.

Individual sales. Berrett-Koehler publications are available through most bookstores. They can also be ordered directly from Berrett-Koehler:
Tel: (800) 929-2929; Fax: (802) 864-7626; www.bkconnection.com

Orders for college textbook/course adoption use. Please contact Berrett-Koehler: Tel: (800) 929-2929; Fax: (802) 864-7626.

Orders by U.S. trade bookstores and wholesalers. Please contact Ingram Publisher Services, Tel: (800) 509-4887; Fax: (800) 838-1149; E-mail: customer.service@ingrampublisherservices.com; or visit www .ingrampublisherservices.com/Ordering for details about electronic ordering.

Berrett-Koehler and the BK logo are registered trademarks of Berrett-Koehler Publishers, Inc.

Printed in the United States of America

Berrett-Koehler books are printed on long-lasting acid-free paper. When it is available, we choose paper that has been manufactured by environmentally responsible processes. These may include using trees grown in sustainable forests, incorporating recycled paper, minimizing chlorine in bleaching, or recycling the energy produced at the paper mill.

Production Management: Michael Bass Associates
Cover Design: The Book Designers

Library of Congress Cataloging-in-Publication Data
Names: Miller, Mark, 1959– author.
Title: Leaders made here : building a leadership culture / Mark Miller, Bestselling Author of Chess, Not Checkers and The Heart of Leadership.
Description: First Edition. | Oakland, CA : Berrett-Koehler Publishers, Inc., [2017]
Identifiers: LCCN 2016048824 | ISBN 9781626569812 (hardcover)
Subjects: LCSH: Leadership.
Classification: LCC HD57.7 .M5377 2017 | DDC 658.4/092--dc23
LC record available at https://lccn.loc.gov/2016048824

First Edition
22 21—20 19 18 17   10 9 8 7 6 5 4 3 2 1

MAR 2 2 2023

This book is dedicated to my wife, Donna. Her patience with me is unfathomable and her contributions to my life are incalculable. I love you!

Contents

 **Introduction**

Leadership is the cornerstone of all great organizations.

Yes, before you think it, I do understand that more is required than outstanding leadership to build an enduring organization. After a five-year research effort, our team found High Performance Organizations actually have *four things* in common. They all Bet on Leadership, Act as One, Win the Heart, and Excel at Execution. I wrote about these "moves" in my previous book, *Chess Not Checkers.*

However, the journey to high performance always begins with leadership. This book is a deep dive on one critical question every organization faces:

How do you ensure you'll have the needed leaders to fuel your future success?

The answer, in short: Build a leadership culture.

Let's be clear on terms from the beginning. A leadership culture exists when leaders are routinely and systematically developed, *and* you have a surplus of leaders ready for the next opportunity or challenge.

Imagine what would happen if organizations were proactive and strategic and built their own leadership pipeline and filled their bench with capable, ready-now leaders? What if companies and nonprofits created a culture in which exceptional leadership at all levels was the norm?

Even as I write this, I am well aware of the resistance to this idea of building a leadership culture. Here are some of the more common objections. . . .

"We don't need a leadership culture; we're doing fine."

You may be right: you are doing fine—for now. However, even in organizations currently enjoying success, this is often due to the efforts of a few good women and men who shoulder the burden for their entire organization. Their heroic acts are required again and again to win the day. Not only does this approach fail to leverage the full capacity of your people, but sustained greatness is unlikely.

"Leaders are born, not made."

If you fall victim to this myth, your organization is probably not going to make the investments needed to grow leaders at all levels. You will just wait for the next leader to walk through the door. In essence, you are waiting for Superman or Superwoman to miraculously appear and save your company. This is a dubious strategy for future success.

"We're too busy to think about the future."

If your organization is like most, you probably do not have enough capable leaders in place today. And, if you have a shortage of leaders, the ones you do have are often pedaling hard just trying to keep up. They certainly aren't thinking about developing future leaders. Therefore, a leadership shortfall today is often the preamble to a shortage of future leaders. If you do not break this cycle, it may ultimately break you.

"Even if we wanted a leadership culture, we don't know how to build one."

This is the best form of resistance! Although I will work to address all the objections outlined above, *Leaders Made Here* was written primarily for this final group—those who can see the value in a strong bench of capable leaders but just lack the strategic framework to make it so. This book is really for you.

Ultimately, your future success depends on the *quantity* and *quality* of leaders on your team. Follow the path outlined in the following pages, and you will position your organization among the elite. You will create a place where leadership excellence is not a dream but rather a by-product of a sound strategy executed with diligence.

The future begins today. Let's get started!

Human Error

The sound was deafening and the confusion was debilitating. Blake was struggling to pick himself up off the floor and wondering what had just happened. The only light streamed in through a small window near the ceiling as the sun crawled over the horizon.

As Blake strained to scan the room, he could see others getting up. They were all covered in dust and debris. His ears were still ringing from the explosion.

Just a moment before, he was beginning his first meeting with his leadership team as the new CEO and then, this. . . .

"Is everyone okay?" Blake yelled.

"I'm okay," came a voice though the shadows.

"Me, too," said another.

A third voice asked, "What happened?"

"I don't know," Blake said, as smoke began to fill the room. "We need to leave the building—now! Where's David . . . and Sally?"

Becky shouted, "They're over here!"

Blake jumped across the table to find both of them on the floor. He leaned over and from what he could see, it didn't look good. They were both unconscious.

"Are they okay?" Amanda screamed.

"I don't know, but we've got to get them out of here," Blake said. "Tim, you and Bill take Sally, and I'll get David."

Luckily, the group had only one flight of stairs to navigate to reach the street level. When they emerged, they found many of their fellow employees had already found their way out of the building. Thankfully, the sound of sirens could be heard getting closer.

Blake and his team laid Sally and David on the grass. David began to cough and sat up; Sally didn't—she wasn't breathing. Blake started administering CPR—no response. Blake continued until the paramedics arrived and took over. They were able to restart Sally's heart and whisk her away to the local hospital.

The employees on the street watched as their building was engulfed in flames. The bright orange flames battled with the rising sun as smoke billowed hundreds of feet into the air. The heat pushed everyone back as several fire engines appeared on site.

Blake approached a man he thought was the plant foreman and said, "Did everyone make it out?"

Regrettably, he said, "I don't think so."

"Who's missing?" Blake demanded.

"We have six team members unaccounted for, sir."

■ ■ ■

Two weeks had gone by since Blake's fateful first morning on the job. The explosion had marked him and the entire organization forever. They had, indeed, lost six lives that morning. The cause was reported to be "human error."

This tragedy compounded the challenge Blake faced. He had been brought in to turn around a struggling company. Now he had to manage the grieving process, rebuild trust, physically rebuild the building, and along the way, change a culture of hideously low engagement and diminishing performance.

As he drove toward the temporary office they had constructed on site, he reflected on the last decade of his life—an emotional, challenging, and fulfilling journey.

After learning to lead during his tenure at Dynastar, the last few years as CEO of a small business had helped him understand what leading an organization demanded. His initiative to teach his entire staff to play chess, not checkers had revolutionized their business. The success they earned had catapulted their performance and market share, and the sustained superior performance brought Blake his share of recognition.

The attention, fueled by a couple of magazine articles, landed Blake on the radar of several executive search firms. In the beginning, he didn't take their calls, but one day he decided to return a call. After hearing an offer that seemed too good to be true, he and his wife Megan decided the upside of this new opportunity was worth the hassle of a move.

Blake's new company was a mid-sized firm in a slow-growth industry. However, his organization was not enjoying any growth; sales were actually declining, and profits were not far behind. Also, he had learned the last engagement survey reflected declining morale as well. He knew these indicators were the result of deeper root causes. He just needed to figure out what they were—and quickly.

Today's meeting would be a challenge. There was a lot to do before the accident; the list of pressing issues was now staggeringly long. The attendees would be the same as two weeks earlier with one exception:

> Becky Gonzales, Sales & Marketing
> Tim Godfrey, Manufacturing
> David Baldwin, Operations
> Bill Alexander, Chief Legal Counsel
> Amanda Chesterfield, Chief Financial Officer

The notable absentee was Sally Danbury, the former head of Human Resources. After what happened, she decided to take an early retirement and spend more time with her grandchildren. After thirty years in the workforce, she felt like she'd earned a break.

"Good morning," Blake said in a tone more subdued than usual.

The team acknowledged his greeting but said nothing.

"How are you?" Blake said addressing the entire group.

A few people expressed their still-raw emotions regarding the accident. David Baldwin, head of Operations, gave a report on the cause of the explosion and presented some process changes being implemented to improve safety in the future.

"That's fine," Blake added, "but I think the solution may be much more difficult than what you just presented."

"What do you mean?" David asked.

"We certainly need the highest safety standards. We must rebuild the trust of our people, and these process changes will help, but as I understand it, the safety measures we had in place before the accident would have worked—if they had been followed. Is that correct?"

"Yes sir, that is correct," David admitted.

"Ladies and gentlemen, this incident is a graphic and tragic indicator of our problem. To call what happened 'human error' is a disgrace to those who died; the root cause would be more accurately labeled 'leadership error.' Leadership failed and people died.

"Based on the last engagement survey data, the vast majority of our people are sleepwalking through their days! This is not an HR problem; it is not the front-line supervisors' fault, and it's certainly not the employees who created this toxic work environment. This is a leadership issue—it is our responsibility.

Leaders are responsible for the culture in an organization. We will raise the bar.

Leaders are responsible for the culture in an organization.

"A decade from now, we will look back on what happened here as both a tragedy and a turning point. We'll create a better organization as a result. I wish we could have changed before it came to this point, but we are where we are.

"For today's meeting, let's hear a quick report on how the plant situation is going to affect the business over the next 90 days and look at the impact on our annual projections," Blake said.

After the final report, Blake said, "I have one more item on our agenda for today. We need to talk about who will take Sally's place as head of HR. Any thoughts?"

Nothing from the group—not a word. Impatiently, Blake asked, "You guys have been talking about succession planning, haven't you?"

Becky spoke for the group, "Well, I'm sorry to say, no; no, we haven't."

"OK," Blake said in disbelief. "I'll do some homework and we'll address the Human Resources issue during our next meeting."

"Anything else?" Bill asked.

"Yes, one more thing," Blake said. "At our next meeting, come prepared to talk about *your* leadership bench. I know now may not feel like the best time to tackle this topic, but if we're not careful, the present will always press out the future. As senior leaders, we must work on both today and tomorrow."

As if choreographed, the group all began to fidget. Blake picked up on it right away. "What did I say?"

"First, can you tell us what you mean by a leadership bench?" Amanda requested.

"Sure, I apologize—that may be new language for you guys. A leadership bench is a term to talk about current and emerging leaders. It is often represented in a plan that outlines your best thinking regarding succession—everyone's 'next man/woman up' strategy and the replacement's replacement as well. Ultimately, I want us to be three deep in every key leadership position."

"I hate to tell you, Blake, but we have nothing like that." Becky seemed to have revealed herself as the spokesperson for the group or at least its most outspoken member.

"Okay, that will be one of the topics on the next agenda. We may need to extend the meeting. We have a lot to talk about. Please bring what you have regarding your current and emerging leaders."

Immediately after the meeting, Blake decided he had enough information to contact his mentor, Jack Deluca. Jack had been a wildly successful CEO, and Blake thought a conversation would be helpful.

Bet on Leadership

Blake sent Jack an email and was not surprised by the response: *See you Thursday morning at 10:00—usual location.*

As Blake had done many times before, he made the drive to Gresham Park. From his new address, on the other side of the state, the drive was a little shorter. Blake knew the routine—find the crowd, and he would find Jack.

Just as on other visits, Blake found the table at which Jack was holding court, schooling some unsuspecting opponent on the finer points of the game of chess. The pristine, fall weather seemed to have increased the crowd of onlookers.

"Checkmate," Jack said in a tone reflecting both excitement and humility. He had won again as he most often did here in the park; grandmasters don't have many legitimate rivals in this setting. The crowd offered what might be described as a "chess clap"—a golf clap but slightly more subdued.

As the latest student left the table wondering what had just happened, and how it happened so quickly,

Jack addressed the crowd, "That's it for today. Thanks for stopping by. See you next week."

As soon as he had finished speaking, he stepped toward Blake and gave him a big hug. "How are you?"

"Good, not great—better now. It's fantastic to see you," Blake said.

"Sit down, sit down. I heard about the accident. Are you okay?"

"Shaken, for sure. Actually, if I'm honest . . . devastated. Jack, six people died! Six of *my* employees."

"I understand, but, Blake, it was your first day on the job. You're good, but you're not that good. There's no way you could have prevented this tragedy. But . . ." Jack paused. "You know you can prevent the next one."

"I hope so," Blake said.

"Hope is not a strategy." This was not the first time Jack had reminded Blake of this truth.

Hope is not a strategy.

"You know what to do."

"Yes, I do. I should lead."

"Damn right—you should lead! Anything else? Are we done here?" Jack asked.

"I just wanted to test a couple of assumptions as I begin this journey."

"Okay, since you're here."

"I know there are four moves that enable high performance: Bet on Leadership, Act as One, Win the Hearts, and Excel at Execution."

"Correct. Those haven't changed."

"I just want to be sure I do this right."

"What do you mean?"

"I don't want to screw this up. My last company was tiny compared to this one. There was no media coverage of my last assignment!" Blake paused, "And, now the accident. . . . This feels different."

"The scope, scale, and complexity may be different, but the way forward is not. When you refer to 'doing this right,' you need to get that out of your head. The four moves work every time. However, how you apply them, the actual tactics, will be determined by the circumstances you face."

"Okay. I thought that's what you would say."

"What's your plan?" Jack asked.

"Well, in addition to providing counseling for all the employees, and physically rebuilding a large portion of the plant, I plan to continue learning all I can about the business and the people, and I'm going to Bet on Leadership."

"Why?"

"I know if we don't crack the code on the leadership challenge, we'll never execute on the other moves. And, as far as I could tell during the first couple of weeks, we have virtually no bench strength. The most prominent example is Sally, the former head of

HR. After the accident, she decided not to return, and it doesn't appear as though we have anyone to fill her seat from the inside."

"Are you sure?"

"Sure of what?"

"Sure no one inside can step up?"

"No, I'm not. I've only been on board two weeks, and it's been a little bit crazy!"

"Well, I would suggest you try an interim, even a consultant, until you're sure. If your instincts are correct and you don't have anyone inside, you can always go outside."

"Got it. I may call you and ask for another meeting."

"I hope you will; it's always great to see you. Please tell Megan and the kids I said hello."

"Any parting wisdom?"

"Have fun—don't let this hard season steal your joy."

On the drive back to the office, Blake thought about Jack's advice to appoint an interim or hire a consultant to help with the leadership bench issue to give him time to learn more about the talent he already had within the organization. As his mind scrolled through the most talented HR people he knew on the planet, one name rose to the top.

Second Chance

She was gone. The most engaging, spirited, caring, and beautiful woman Charles had ever known had just slipped away. He had lost not only his wife and the mother of their child, but his soulmate. He was numb.

Tears began to roll down Charles's face as he stared at the bank of machines that had been trying to extend Ann's life. They had failed, and Charles was listening to a sound he would never forget. Ann's monitor was broadcasting the lifeless tone of a heart no longer beating. Would it start again? He knew the answer was no. Not this time.

Many would say Ann had already cheated death. Her diagnosis had given her only months to live, but she was a fighter and had turned months into years. Now, her time was up—no miracle cure, no new treatment, no more experimental drugs. She was really gone.

Charles and Ann had been married only six years; her illness had taken its toll on both of them. Charles looked, and felt, much older than his birthdate on his driver's license. In some ways, Ann's passing lifted a tremendous weight—the pain, the waiting, the unknown. These issues were, in part, resolved now but replaced with a new set of realities. In the moment, the burden felt even heavier.

Charles's mind raced at a dizzying pace. How would he tell Samantha, their four-year-old daughter? She had known for a long time her mom was sick, but how would she respond to Ann's death? What would she do without a mother? Who would take care of her? Charles's job took him literally around the world. Would he have to get a new job?

Charles thought, "I need a drink." Unfortunately, he had said those words many times during Ann's illness. The truth was, he couldn't stop drinking even if he wanted to. Ann's death had just compounded his very complicated life.

■ ■ ■

By the time Blake reached his office, he had decided to take Jack's advice and bring in someone to help on an interim basis. He knew the myriad of problems the organization was facing were probably attributable to the way they thought about their people and, more specifically, leadership. He knew of one person who could help him out of this mess—Charles Jones.

Blake and Charles's relationship went way back. Charles was a rock star in the human resources world, but he was a leader first and foremost. Charles was a college friend and had been in Blake and Megan's wedding. Blake realized he regretted losing touch with Charles. The last he had heard Charles had taken a job as the head of Global Human Resources for a huge firm based in London. He knew he had to give him a call.

Blake cleared his calendar the next morning, and after a couple of calls and emails, he found out how to reach Charles. He placed the call.

"Charles, Blake Brown here. Remember me? I knew you before you were a global phenom. Man, it's good to talk to you!"

Charles did not respond. "Charles, are you there? Can you hear me?"

"Yes, Blake. It's good to hear from you."

"I'm sorry we lost touch. I know we've both been too busy," Blake said, his energy still gushing. "How are you? And Ann and Samantha?"

"Well, . . . "

"Charles, are you okay?" Blake asked.

"No, Blake. No, I'm not."

"What's wrong?"

"I don't know where to start." There was a long pause. "Ann died a few months ago."

"No! I'm so sorry."

"And, Sam. . . ." Charles stopped. "What about Sam?" Blake was almost afraid to ask. "Is she okay?"

"She's with my parents. I haven't seen her much in the last few months."

"Why is she with your parents?"

"I'm an alcoholic, and my parents have been keeping her while I've been in treatment."

"Man. . . ." Blake didn't know what to say. He timidly asked, "How about work?"

"I'm on a leave of absence, but I'm not sure I'm going back."

"Why not?"

"The travel. Ultimately, I need to be home with Sam—now more than ever. She wants a pony, and I want not only to give her one, I want to be there when she rides it."

After a long silence, Blake asked, "How is the treatment going?"

"Good, I think. They've encouraged me to count the days. I've been sober for 94 days."

"That sounds like great progress. What are your next steps?"

"I finished the resident phase this week. Now, I think I'll start looking for a new job. Then, I'm going to rebuild my life."

"Maybe I can help," Blake offered.

"How?"

"That's why I called. I need the world's best HR guy to help me turn around my organization. Are you game?"

"Are you kidding? Why do you think I'm your guy after all I just told you?" Charles said in disbelief.

"You are the guy regardless of what you just told me. Besides, it sounds like you are ready to get back to work—I have plenty of that for you. How about a one-year consulting engagement? You said Sam is with your parents. Don't they live near here?"

"They do, but I'm not sure I'm ready to take care of Sam."

"That's your decision. I was just thinking being here is one more benefit of this situation. Don't think of it as a career move—consider it a transition play."

"I'll take it."

"That was too easy."

"You got me with the Sam connection."

"Any other questions for now?" Blake asked.

"No, I'll do it. We'll figure out the details. Thank you!" Charles exclaimed. Here was a real gift—a chance to reboot his life and get back on track. He was sure he could help Blake and his team win big, regardless of their problems.

"I am so sorry about your situation," Blake said. "I just want to say, I'll help you any way I can. Just let me know. I'm excited to have you on this project. I think it will be a chance for you to get back on your feet and help our company do the same. Thanks for your willingness to help us. Can you start next week?"

"You name the time and place and I'll be there!" Charles said with a heart filled with gratitude and excitement—he was back in the game.

The Assignment

Charles and Blake agreed on a time and place for their first meeting, two hours before Blake's next leadership team meeting. He wanted to give Charles a little more context before he met the team.

During their meeting, Blake did a great job establishing the facts as he understood them, acknowledging he was still fairly new. Blake and Charles both understood they were operating on numerous assumptions at this point. Part of Charles's role would be to validate or dismiss these and try to determine what was really happening in the organization.

"This was very helpful," Charles said. "You answered most of my questions."

"Yeah, but I think I said, 'I don't know' a lot." Both men laughed.

"Agreed. But it's always good to know what you don't know. The truth is always better than a bad assumption."

"Are you ready to meet my team?"

"Yes, sir."

"Oh, one more thing, I have scheduled another meeting after this one for us."

"Okay, who will we meet?"

"Your team."

"I didn't know I had a team," Charles grinned.

"The team Sally led before her departure. As the interim head of HR, they're yours."

"Is Sally's replacement in the group?"

The truth is always better than a bad assumption.

"Don't know. I just assumed you would need some help turning this place around."

"No pressure there," Charles smiled.

■ ■ ■

As Blake's team began to gather in the conference room, he introduced Charles to each one but didn't explain his role. After everyone arrived, Blake officially began the meeting.

"Good morning! I hope you had a fantastic weekend. I usually like to begin meetings with some personal join-up time, but this morning, let's focus on a professional update.

"Each of you met Charles when you arrived. He is one of the finest HR professionals on the planet. He and I have known each other for years. When Sally left, I decided to invite Charles to help us. He will be serving as our interim HR leader. Ultimately, he'll also help us find Sally's replacement. Let's jump-start

Charles's time with us by telling him a little about what each of you do."

The next hour flew by. Charles took copious notes as one by one the members of the team shared their stories. People love to talk about themselves, so this time proved extremely valuable for both Blake and Charles.

Then, Blake turned to Charles and said, "Why don't you tell them about some of your work?" Blake had been purposeful in not taking the conversation into personal topics during this first meeting. He didn't want to put any undue pressure on Charles to share his story, for which Charles was very appreciative. Instead, he told about the work he and his team had completed at his previous company and his most recent work on a global scale.

When Charles was finished, Blake added, "And, Charles has been recognized as a global thought leader on leadership development by numerous groups. In addition to the work for his firm, he is a sought-after speaker and he's also written a couple of books. He probably wouldn't tell you that part." Blake smiled. "Thanks for your willingness to help us."

"My pleasure," Charles said.

"Now, regarding our agenda for today. I know I'm new here, but based on our previous meetings and numerous individual conversations, I've reached one conclusion, and it's where I've asked Charles to start. We need a leadership culture." Blake stopped to let that sink in a moment.

Becky looked around the table and, as usual, was the first to speak, "What does that mean, exactly?"

Blake went to the board and wrote as he spoke:

> ## A leadership culture exists when leaders are routinely and systematically developed, AND when you have a surplus of leaders.

Blake turned to the group and said, "We want more and better leaders."

Charles was trying to read the room for reactions as the men and women at the table sat there staring at the whiteboard.

"Thoughts? Reactions?" Blake asked.

"Why would we want that? We already have leaders. We *are* the leaders. Why do we want any more?" Amanda asked.

"Well, there are numerous reasons," Charles said. "We can improve our performance and be better positioned to create the future we desire. The only thing limiting our future is the number of leaders we can develop. It will also help when leaders transition—like Sally."

Blake jumped in, "Exactly. The reason we don't appear to have anyone to take Sally's place is that we don't have a culture that is focused on building leaders."

"What do you mean by 'culture'?" Tim asked.

Blake turned to Charles. "Why don't you answer this one?"

"Sure. A culture is nothing more than the sum of the habits of the people. Culture is not what you want it to be—it is what people *do* on a regular basis. So, if you routinely and systematically develop leaders, it is part of your culture.

"What about the surplus idea? Seems wasteful to me," Amanda added.

Blake added, "That's the test. If you have a surplus, the process is working. If you don't have a surplus, you have a shortfall. The shortfall is what we want to eliminate."

"Where do we begin?" Becky asked hesitantly. Again, Blake looked at Charles. He took the handoff.

"Well, the good news first: Building a leadership culture is doable. It will require some time and diligence on our part, but much of the design work can be executed by the HR professionals on Sally's former team."

"So, we can delegate this?" Amanda was suggesting more than asking.

"Not exactly; sorry if I got your hopes up." Charles chuckled; no one else did. "Building a leadership culture will need to be one of your strategic priorities for the foreseeable future. It won't happen without your direct involvement and support."

"What do we do?" Bill asked.

"Today, we're going to do a simple exercise to kick off our work." Charles distributed 3 × 5 cards and asked each member of the team to write the organization's definition of leadership on the card and pass it back in.

Three minutes later, Charles collected the cards and read each one aloud—an eye-opening experience for the group. Some of the definitions were really good; others were downright confusing. When he finished reading the last card, Charles addressed the group.

"These are all wonderful definitions of leadership," he said, exaggerating just a little. "What do you notice about them?"

Becky said, "They are all *very* different."

"Yes, and that's our first issue. What problems do you think this could create for us as an organization?"

Charles captured the team's comments:

Pitfalls of Multiple Definitions of Leadership

- Not knowing who and where to recruit
- Different selection criteria
- Multiple training agendas across departments
- Inconsistent recognition
- Inconsistent rewards
- Employee morale issues
- Difficulty moving leaders from department to department
- Wasted energy across the organization
- Inefficient process for evaluation and development
- No common language
- Differing expectations for leaders

"To create a leadership culture, we must forge a common definition of leadership. If we all operate with different definitions, we'll never reach our full potential," Charles said.

"So . . . ?" Tim asked.

"Our first step is to work on a common definition," Charles said.

"Who's the 'our' in that statement?" Amanda asked.

"My next meeting is with Sally's former team. Defining our leadership point of view will be the first item on the agenda. We'll come back with a recommendation."

"Any questions?" Blake asked. Although there were many, no one wanted to offer them in the moment. Hearing no response, Blake said, "Thanks for your support as we move forward. This is going to help us in the short run and for years to come. Thanks to you, Charles, for helping us work through these important issues."

Our Point of View

The next meeting was with Charles's new team. The group was small—only four of them, and as Charles would soon learn, they were competent but lacked strategic direction.

Blake called the meeting to order and greeted everyone. "Thanks for allowing me to crash your meeting today. I know Sally talked to you about her decision. Today, I want to tell you how we're going to move forward.

"I've asked Charles Jones to join us as your interim leader and to help us during the transition. Ultimately, he will help us find Sally's replacement. For now, I've asked him to work with you to begin the process of creating a leadership culture." Blake continued with a brief bio including some of Charles's recognition in the field. A couple of the team members already knew Charles by reputation.

"I know you have a lot of questions. Before we dive into those, I want Charles to get to know you a little better. Let's introduce ourselves and share some of the work you've been doing."

Each member of the team shared a brief work history as Blake had requested, but the conversation also took a very personal tone. As with the earlier meeting, Blake had intended to steer the conversation toward work, but the team had other ideas. Apparently, this was a reflection of Sally's efforts to build genuine community among the team members.

Charles learned Rose's mom had just moved in with her, Gary and his wife were expecting their first child, Kim was continuing her education online, and Bob was passionate about gardening. On his turn, he swallowed hard and said, "Hi, I'm Charles, and I am an alcoholic." A couple of the group snickered, thinking he was making a joke.

"No, really. I figure I might as well tell you the truth up front. However, I am in recovery. I've also had some other hard things in my life recently, but I'll save those for another day."

"I'm sorry I laughed," Rose said.

"That's okay. I know you weren't expecting a recovering addict to join your team."

The group was all about radical transparency, but they weren't quite sure what to do with this. Finally, Bob said, "Well, Charles, there are no perfect people here. We're glad you're doing better. Let us know if we can help."

"Thanks, Bob," Charles said, attempting to hold back his emotions. This was the first time he had

admitted his problem outside his recovery group. The
moment brought a flood of feelings and emotions—
embarrassment, fear, loneliness, grief and more.
The pain was almost unbearable. He missed Ann
and Sam. Maintaining his composure, he said again,
"Thank you.

"On a lighter note," Charles added, smiling, "I'm
excited about the work Blake has asked us to do
together. It should be a lot of fun."

"I'm glad you circled back to that," Rose said.
"What exactly is a leadership culture, why would
we want one and assuming we do, how would we
build one?"

"Whoa! Thanks, Rose. I heard several questions
there. Let me start with the why would we want a
leadership culture question. Blake, speak up if I miss
anything.

"Blake and I both believe leadership is the only
sustainable competitive advantage. Therefore, if you
can create a culture in which growing leaders is part
of your DNA, you can always position yourself to win.
Great organizations always Bet on Leadership."

"Exactly what does a 'leadership culture' look
like?" asked Kim, the newest member of the team.

"The culture of any organization is nothing
more than the consistent behaviors of its members,"
Charles said. "As an example, it seems to me, serving
others is part of your culture. Would you agree?"

The team nodded in agreement.

"It's part of your culture, not because you say it is, but because you actually live it out on a daily basis. Every employee looks for opportunities to serve others inside your team, the staff at large, and your community. Serving has become a cultural norm. It's not seen as an extracurricular activity but is embraced as a part of everyone's role. Therefore, it is part of your culture."

The culture of any organization is nothing more than the consistent behaviors of its members.

"So how does that same logic apply to the concept of a leadership culture?" Gary asked.

"Here's the way Blake and I described it for his team this morning:

A leadership culture exists when leaders are routinely and systematically developed and you have a surplus of leaders."

"I get the routinely and systematically part, but why the idea of a surplus?" Kim asked.

"The surplus of talented, skilled, and 'ready-now' leaders would be our indication we are winning. Without a surplus, we would forever be in catch-up mode," Charles said.

Blake picked up the response. "Leadership is critical to our future success. It is like oxygen—without it, you die. As an organization, we don't want to wonder where our next breath is coming from."

"We've been training leaders," Bob said.

"Yes, and we'll continue to do so, but I believe our assignment, and our future, is to help create a leadership culture, not just offer a few optional training classes for leaders," Charles responded.

"How do you do that?" Gary asked.

"Let's begin to answer your question by reviewing a draft of a charter. I've not shared this with Blake or his team yet. I wanted each of you to see it, and together, let's make any needed changes before we roll up our sleeves and get to work."

"That's my cue," Blake said as he stood to leave. "I look forward to seeing your recommendations. Call on me if I can help."

"Thank you for your vision," Charles said.

As Blake left, Charles said, "Let's get started."

Leadership Culture Project

TEAM CHARTER

Purpose

Create long-term, sustainable competitive advantage and improved performance through the creation of a leadership culture. *A leadership culture exists when leaders are routinely and systematically developed and you have a surplus.*

Key Deliverables

Identify the systems, practices, mechanisms, and activities that will enable us to create a leadership culture and a preliminary budget required to begin the journey.

Design Principles

- Create a process/framework/strategy that applies to leaders at all levels—from new supervisors to senior leaders.

- Clearly communicate individual leaders must take responsibility for their own development.

- Plan for a highly customized process—one size will not fit all.

- Determine ways to intentionally engage emerging leaders in the process.

- Solicit input from across the organization during the development phases of this project.

- Incorporate global best practices

Budget

Recommendations will be submitted to the senior team on March 15.

Success Metrics

To be determined

Sponsor

Blake Brown

The team spent an hour asking questions about the charter and the work it described. They were keenly interested in the details.

"Will there be training? Who will deliver the training?"

"What are the budget implications for next year and beyond?"

"Can we hire additional staff?"

"What role will the senior leaders play?"

"What would the communications plan entail?"

Charles, in an attempt to corral the conversation, responded, "These are all fantastic questions. My general answer is, I don't know. You're asking the type of questions we have the opportunity to answer *together.* The answers will be our recommendations—they will be the product of the charter."

"What's our next step?" Kim asked.

"Well, I had planned to share this draft with Blake and his team for their input at their next meeting," Charles said.

Kim responded, "That sounds like a good idea. What's next on our agenda today?"

"One more item," Charles said. In an effort to determine how aligned the team was on the issue, Charles repeated the 3 × 5 card activity he had done earlier.

Sixty seconds after Charles handed out the cards, he noticed everyone was finished. This seemed odd to Charles given what he had seen earlier with Blake's team. When he collected the cards, much to Charles's surprise, every member of the team had written the same definition of leadership!

How is this possible? He thought.

"This is quite impressive. All of you have written the same definition," Charles said.

"Thanks," Bob said, on behalf of the group. "We've been working really hard on forging a common definition of leadership for several months. Sally was convinced its absence was limiting our impact."

"This is fantastic! I agree with Sally. There's just one *big* problem," Charles paused.

"And that is?" Rose asked.

"I did this same exercise with Blake's team this morning, and all their answers were different. They don't know your definition! Unfortunately, as long as the senior leaders don't embrace the same definition of leadership, we'll never create a leadership culture."

The team laughed. Kim spoke first. "It's okay, Charles. We have not shared our conclusions and recommendations with the senior team yet. The fact they have different answers is perfect. Maybe that will help us create the case for a common definition."

"Let's talk more about your definition. I see 'Great Leaders SERVE' on your cards, but give me the context and the backstory," Charles said.

"Before we tell you, we should offer a disclaimer," Gary began. "We do not believe there is one universal best way to define leadership. However, we have concluded that as an organization, we need *one common definition.*"

"That's exactly what I told Blake's team this morning," Charles added.

"One more bit of context," Kim chimed in. "There are a lot of great definitions out there. Some are simple, others complex; some are academic, and others quite conceptual. We decided we wanted something actionable."

"And we needed a picture," Rose added.

"And?" Charles's curiosity was about to get the best of him.

Kim stood up and went to the whiteboard. "First, the picture." She drew the following:

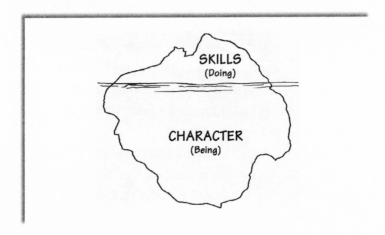

"Our picture of leadership is an iceberg," Kim continued, "about 10 percent above the waterline and 90 percent below. The part below represents leadership character. The 10 percent above the water represents the skills or competencies of the leader— what she or he actually does.

"When we consider what leaders *do*, we believe they all serve." As she explained each practice, she wrote them on the flipchart:

See the Future

Engage and Develop Others

Reinvent Continuously

Value Results and Relationships

Embody the Values

"Because service is part of our culture, it was a small step to think about how the best leaders SERVE. It was an idea Sally learned from a mentor she worked with in the past. I think her name was Debbie."

"Great leaders SERVE. Yes, I get it now. Anything else?" Charles asked.

"Yes, there is a lot more," Bob responded. "The 90% below the waterline—leadership character—is a *big* deal. Our plan to is to include it in our selection criteria for future leaders. Later, we'll also work on how to help our current leaders strengthen their leadership character."

"This is tremendous!" Charles added. "I told the team this morning that to create a leadership culture the first step is to agree on a common definition. It looks like you have already done outstanding work on this. Okay, what's next?"

"We thought you would tell us," Kim smiled.

Charles responded, "I look forward to figuring out our next steps together!"

■ ■ ■

Charles was glad he and Blake had scheduled a series of short meetings to be sure Blake was informed of the team's progress as well as their challenges. Today was the first of those sessions.

"I think we are off to a fantastic start," Charles said.

"What makes you say that?"

"The fact the team already has a solid definition of leadership," Charles said. "Did you know they had worked on one?"

"No, I didn't," Blake admitted.

"Neither did your leaders," Charles smiled. "At some point, we'll need to see if you and your team can support what they've come up with."

"Agreed." Blake was optimistic. "How can we keep our team involved in the process moving forward?

"I plan to ask for their input on the charter at our next meeting," Charles offered.

"That sounds good. What else can we do?" Blake asked.

"I think some one-on-one meetings will be important."

"I really want to win them over," Blake said.

"Got it."

"You know you have a few skeptics on the senior team?"

"I assumed we would. Someone from my team will spend time with each of them individually during the process. We will also do frequent updates with the entire team together. If you think anything else is needed, please let me know."

⚒ That's My Job

During Blake's next team meeting, Charles shared the draft of the charter to scores of questions. The level of skepticism was high, but Blake was clear: creating a leadership culture was at the top of his strategic agenda. The charter was approved.

In his next team meeting, Charles began by telling the team the charter had been approved by Blake and the senior team. Next, he asked them how they wanted to proceed. An extended discussion concluded with the following:

Action Items

- Talk to key stakeholders within the company about leadership development—starting with Blake's leadership team members
- Find secondary research on companies that excel at developing leaders

- Compile a list of the current activities underway in the arena of leadership development across the organization
- Create a short list of companies that would be willing to host a benchmark visit from the team

The conversation then turned to their key stakeholder interviews, and the team began to discuss the questions they would like to ask. Basically, they decided to ask open-ended questions about leadership development to explore what these leaders felt had worked in the past and to ask for suggestions concerning the future. Their questions included the following:

- What contributed to *your* growth as a leader?
- What characteristics do you look for when attempting to identify emerging leaders?
- Which activities do you generally find most helpful in fostering the growth of an emerging leader?
- How do you monitor the growth of leaders on your team?
- What advice do you have for us as we try to create a leadership culture?

The focus for the interviews: LISTEN, and take good notes.

Charles concluded, "It sounds like we have a plan. Let's get started."

■ ■ ■

The team divided up the interview assignments. Rose would be visiting with David Baldwin, head of Operations. Everyone knew he was one of the longest-tenured employees at their company and a "self-made" leader. Some were concerned he might be resistant to new ways of doing things.

"Hi, David. Thanks for carving out some time to meet with me," Rose said.

"Listen, we need to make this quick. I don't have time to meet with you. I was told I had to. So, let's cut to the chase: I don't support whatever you're trying to do."

"Okay. . . ." Rose hadn't even sat down yet. She was immediately searching for what to say next when David said, "You don't need to sit down. I think we are done. We had our meeting."

"David, do you even know what it is we are trying to do?"

"As I understand it, you are trying to do *my job*."

"Absolutely not," Rose protested.

"You're on a team working to create a leadership culture, whatever that is. Am I correct?"

"Yes."

"Well, I am responsible for the culture in my area—not you or Charles or even Blake."

"I understand completely," Rose offered in response. "However, we are going to need a lot more leaders at all levels to create the future we want."

"I develop my own leaders," David said gruffly.

"Yes, and I believe you have numerous open leadership positions at the moment. And, you have no qualified internal candidates."

"Your point?" David's tone softened a bit based on the fact Rose had done her homework and spotted a weak spot in his "process" for developing leaders.

"All we are trying to do is help you, and all our leaders, strengthen your leadership bench. We believe we will always need a blend of inside and outside leadership hires. We just don't want to be forced to make all our leadership selections from the outside."

"I have qualified people. . . ."

Before he could continue, Rose added, "All I know is several of your 'qualified people' have been rejected for higher levels of leadership." She stopped to let the thought sink in and then said, "All we want to do is help."

"If I need your help, which I doubt, I will call you. We are done here," David said as he walked out of his office leaving Rose standing there, thinking, *That went well.*" She smiled and went back to her office to capture her notes from the "interview" with David.

Study the Best

As the additional internal interviews were approaching, Charles wanted to be sure Blake and the senior team were comfortable with the team's external benchmarking plans. During their next weekly meeting, Charles raised the subject.

"Game on!" Charles said as he greeted Blake. "We've started our interviews."

"How's that going?" Blake asked.

"Based on a sample of one—very interesting! I will know a lot more after a couple more meetings. No doubt the time will be well invested. Today, I want to tell you about our benchmarking plans and be sure we're in sync on that."

"You know, I'm a big fan of benchmarking," Blake began. "However, in this case, I thought we hired you to give us the answers," he said with a huge smile.

"I could," Charles replied, returning the smile, "but I want to help the team grow in the process. You and I both know benchmarking isn't required to build a leadership culture, but an open mind and a bias for learning are prerequisites. Besides, like you, I have always been a huge fan of studying the best. I think it's one of the ways we combat our own hubris. We can always find someone better at something than we are. Benchmarking done well can really expand our world."

Benchmarking done well can really expand our world.

"I agree. What do you have in mind?"

"Just three or four companies. I promise you, the investment will pay huge dividends. Besides, a couple of trips for each team member will also expand their professional network."

"No concerns from me. I trust your judgment," Blake affirmed.

"Thanks! We will give you a full report from our visits. Who knows what we'll learn?"

"See you soon," Blake stood and shook Charles's hand; he tightened his grip as he said, "I'm thankful you're with us on this. How are *you* doing?"

"Better. There were some scary, sleepless nights; now I'm just battling the loneliness. It's probably a combination of Ann's death, being away from Sam so much, and the recovery journey—they told me I would feel like crap. I often do, so, I guess I'm good."

"Hang on and let me know how I can help."

"Will do," Charles said. As he walked away, he reflected on how thankful he was to have Blake in his life.

■ ■ ■

While additional in-house interviews were scheduled, Kim was working on identifying companies to benchmark. She asked the same question of everyone she approached: If you were building an organization in which leadership development was part of the DNA, who would you study? Interestingly, several organizations were mentioned again and again.

For the final review, Kim teamed up with Gary for a deeper dive on the companies that were surfacing repeatedly. Gary combed the Internet, trade publications, and business literature and purchased several studies produced by third parties profiling these companies. He also reviewed the annual report from all the publicly traded companies.

From Kim and Gary's work, eight companies emerged that seemed to do an excellent job of creating a leadership culture and had outstanding performance over time.

■ ■ ■

At the team's next meeting, Charles was optimistic. As everyone arrived, he could sense the excitement growing.

"How is everyone?" Charles opened the meeting. "Any news on the baby watch?"

"Last weekend, we picked colors for the nursery, bought a stroller, hung a mobile, put the baby bed together; now it's time to paint. I know what I'm doing this weekend. If anyone here wants to help, let me know." Gary was clearly energized by the nesting phase of their journey.

When he finished, without any prodding, Bob reported on the effects of the drought on his plants. Kim added that finals were approaching—she was in "cramming mode." Then, Rose talked about her mother's health and their latest trip to the doctor. And in a final join-up moment, Charles added that he had recently started running for the first time since high school. A recent physical combined with a friend's challenge were enough to get him back on the track.

Kim began the project discussion, "We've found eight potential companies to visit. I've not contacted them, because I wanted to get the group's input on which ones to pursue. I'm guessing based on our schedule we will probably have time to visit three or four of them."

"And," Gary added, "there's no guarantee they'll meet with us."

"Why would they?" Kim said. "If leadership development is part of their competitive advantage, why would they tell us how they do it?"

Charles said, "Gary and Kim, you are both correct; some companies hold their practices very closely. However, because we've taken care to avoid direct competitors, maybe they'll agree to help us. But, who knows what will happen? We'll ask and respond accordingly."

Kim wrote the names of the companies on the whiteboard. The eight were mostly high-profile organizations from diverse industries.

"How do we decide this?" asked Charles.

"Gary, is there anything in your research that might help us?" Rose asked.

"I'm not sure. I was able to confirm that all of them really do the stuff we are looking for. They are very intentional about developing leaders at all levels and are also successful based on the financial data I could find."

Charles looked at the list. "Kim, I have a question for you and Gary. What is the strength of each company? What do they do exceptionally well in the arena of leadership development that should keep them on our radar?"

"Let's figure that out together," Kim offered.

The following discussion revealed the individual strengths of each organization. Because there was some overlap, the team was able to eliminate a couple of the candidates.

In the final analysis, the team decided to contact only three of the domestic organizations and one of the non-U.S.-based firms. They didn't want to naively assume the best the world had to offer would be found in the United States.

Gary took the action item to make the call to these companies. If any of them said no, they would go back to those just removed from the list.

Next on the agenda: *Reports from the Interviews.* At this point, only Rose had completed her interview.

"How was your time with David?" Charles asked.

"Well, . . ." Rose began very slowly. "I think this project is going to be harder than we might have originally thought."

"What are you talking about?" Gary asked.

"My interview with David—it wasn't really an interview. He didn't even let me sit down. He told me he did not support what we are doing, even though he admitted he was unclear what we are actually working on."

"What?" Bob said. "On what grounds?"

"How can the head of Operations be against leadership development?" Kim asked.

"Oh, he's not against leadership development. He's against us, or anyone else, influencing *his* culture. His sense of ownership appears to have crossed from healthy to unhealthy, if you ask me. It felt like a mash-up of paranoia, pride, fear, and control."

"That's not a good mixture," Gary added.

"No, I think it's actually lethal," Rose said. "I mentioned his approach was not working that well. Specifically, I pointed out the open leadership positions in his department and the lack of internal candidates."

"You did not?" Bob was mortified.

"Well, it may not have been the smartest thing I ever did." Rose paused. "He wanted to fight and I fought back. I'm sorry."

"That's okay. The facts are the facts. If David cannot acknowledge the truth, we have another issue to add to our list of concerns," Charles added.

"So, what's next with David?" Gary asked.

"I have no idea," Rose said.

"Let's just be aware of skeptics in high places." Charles added, "We need to find ways to serve them, too. 'Partnership' is the word that comes to mind for me. After all, we are on the same team."

"I'm glad I'm not on his team," Kim said under her breath.

Scale Matters

Gary contacted the benchmark companies and informed the team all had agreed to meet. Two of the four requested a return visit. He was straightforward in his response; he told them a visit at this time would be premature, because they were very early on this journey. He promised to follow up when more had been accomplished. His candor was appreciated and did not thwart any of the team's upcoming visits.

For their first visit, the team decided to send Charles, Bob, and Kim. They agreed not to ask Rose to travel until her mom was more settled.

The first company was a large, well-established, global organization in the financial sector. It had tens of billions in assets and had been successful for a very long time. Although the organization had certainly been impacted by the economics of the day, a conservative posture had served it well during turbulent times.

When the team arrived at the firm's global training facility, they found the place to be well appointed but not flashy—designed to make their usual students, banking and finance professionals, feel comfortable and relaxed. Today the team would meet with Judy Cortez, the executive director charged with leadership development.

Judy's assistant, Marty, greeted the team in the lobby and offered them coffee before escorting them to a small breakout room.

"Judy will be joining you shortly," he said as the group settled in.

Only moments later, Judy, a woman in her mid-50s, dressed in a simple business suit, entered the room.

"Thanks for coming!" Judy said as she shook hands with the team. "We love it when we can have guests."

"Speaking of guests," Bob asked, "how many do you have in a year?"

"We have two categories: students and day guests. Last year we had 9,332 students, but we're ahead of that pace this year. And, we had 64 professionals like you visit last year to study our approach to leadership development," Judy said with a level of precision you would expect at a financial services company.

"This is primarily a teaching campus. We will conduct 227 different courses here this year."

Charles spoke up, "We're getting ahead of ourselves. Let me first thank you again for meeting with us. I would also like to clarify why we're here, introduce ourselves, and then we do have some questions."

"A lot of questions," Bob added.

During the visit, Judy was easy to talk to, and her years in the field provided rich examples.

Near the end of the meeting, Charles said, "We have gained a tremendous amount of insight from you, and we are very appreciative. I'd like to conclude our time with one final question. What would you do differently if you were starting over?"

"I love that question. The truth is we have learned so much, we would do many things differently."

"Can you share a couple?" Bob asked.

"Sure. First, we would have started with agreement on what the word 'leadership' actually means in our organization. There are thousands of definitions out there; we should have chosen one—or created our own. This misstep cost us a lot of time and wasted energy."

"We've made some progress on this, but the reminder is helpful—thank you," Charles said. "What else?"

"We were slow to scale our programming. We should have moved faster."

"What do you mean by 'scale'?" Kim asked. "Based on what we've seen here, it looks like you have scaled."

"Two things: We needed more classes. There's certainly real power in a common definition of leadership; there's even *more* power in a common leadership skillset. Our training is the primary vehicle to help people learn these skills. As an example, when we decided to pursue Six Sigma as a quality improvement strategy, it took us five years to train all our leaders because we didn't have enough classes. We weren't smart. We missed significant dividends by not scaling more quickly.

"We also scaled too slowly for the different levels of leadership. We invested the vast majority of our budget on senior leaders for way too long. Yes, senior leaders need development, but they are also the ones who generally have access to funds, conferences, mentors, executive coaching, and other resources. Junior and emerging leaders often don't have the same opportunities. Today, we provide programming across all leadership levels."

Charles ended the session by saying, "This has been great! Thanks for your openness, and congratulations on all you've accomplished here. This place is amazing!"

That evening over dinner the group debriefed their visit. Bob was the first to comment after the appetizers were ordered. "Today was awesome. I took fifteen pages of notes!"

"I think I beat you," Charles said. "Let me count . . . 17, 18, 19—nineteen pages. Actually, as I look at them, most of my notes are questions."

"Questions? Really? What kind of questions?" Bob asked.

"Generally, questions about translation to our culture. One of the traps we need to avoid is to attempt to superimpose practices that work in one organization but will not work in ours," Charles said.

The team of three had a good dinner and an even better conversation. Bob agreed to email their collective notes back to the rest of the team so everyone could stay in the loop.

The Big Idea

Charles woke before the alarm sounded. His sleep patterns had become tenuous in the previous months. In the midst of it all, he had tried to establish a bit of a routine as part of his path back to normalcy.

After he showered and shaved, he went to a local diner for his usual: scrambled eggs and turkey bacon with wheat toast—no butter. While he was sitting at the counter, someone tapped him on this shoulder. He turned around to see his mom, dad, and Samantha! He was speechless. He hadn't seen Sam in weeks. This was not how he expected to start his day.

Stunned and a bit disoriented by the surprise, Charles regained his composure and said, "Hello! It's so great to see you!"

Bending down on one knee, he gave Sam the biggest hug of her life. He didn't want to let her go. The flood of emotions was overwhelming. Charles began to cry. Through his tears, he looked at Sam and said, "How are you?" She nodded and began to cry herself. She wasn't sure why she was crying, maybe just because her daddy was crying. They hugged again as

Charles scooped her up in his arms. "What are you doing here? Is everything okay?"

"Well, Sam said she needed to see you, and so we called your office to see if we could surprise you. They put us through to a nice young man named Blake. He encouraged us to come here this morning," Charles's dad said.

"He did? Uh," Charles stammered, "I have a trip today. I'm headed on a visit with some of my team."

"Blake said he knew that and would cover for you—he said he cancelled your flight."

"He did?"

"Yes, he seems like a nice young man," his dad added.

"Blake is a great guy. Just let me call the team and tell them what has happened."

"No, that's not necessary," Charles's dad insisted. "Blake said he would take care of everything. He recommended several parks, a couple of restaurants, and a show tonight. He booked our hotel near where you're staying, too. He was better than a travel agent."

"Did we tell you we think he's really nice?" Charles's mom asked.

"You're right—he is an amazing guy." Charles squeezed Sam really tight and said, "Let's go to the park!"

As Charles and his family were headed out on their unexpected day of fun, Blake, Kim, and Gary were about to head out on their own adventure.

■ ■ ■

The flight was scheduled to leave just after 10:00. Kim and Gary were already at the gate when Blake arrived.

"What are you doing here?" Kim asked. "Where's Charles—is everything okay?"

"Yes, Charles is great. He had family show up unexpectedly, and I told him I would cover this trip for him."

"Glad to have you," Gary said.

Just before they boarded, Blake asked Kim to tell him about their destination.

"This company is very different from the first company," she began.

"I guessed that, when I saw the email that said we should dress in business casual," Gary said.

"Yes, business casual is the norm—you'll find this place much less formal than the financial services environment of the first visit. But don't let that deceive you. This, too, is a large global business that is very successful. They are also very serious about helping all their people grow. It's actually part of their employment brand," Kim said.

Gary said, "Explain what you mean by 'employment brand.'"

"Gladly." Kim continued, "An employment brand is similar to any other brand. In its simplest form, a brand is what you want people to think about when they hear your name. Some say a brand is a promise.

As competition for high-caliber employees has increased in recent years, companies like the one we will visit today have decided they should offer more than a paycheck to attract and retain the brightest and best. Part of their employment brand, their promise, is growth and development opportunities for their employees."

"Let's probe this issue today," Blake said. "Based on what I've heard, this approach has given many organizations a real advantage when recruiting top talent. People want more than a paycheck and basic benefits. As far as I am concerned, this is the new normal if you want to attract the brightest and best people."

"Do you think the promise of personal growth can really entice people to work for a company?" Gary asked.

"I think so," Blake said. "Most people do want to grow—especially leaders. Sometimes they may need a little encouragement to combat complacency, but the best leaders are always learners."

When they arrived at their destination, they were planning to rent a car, but their host for the day, Chad Freeman, surprised them by meeting them as they came through the airport.

Chad was in his early 30s, young for a vice president of Operations. He was confident and casual in his jeans and a sweatshirt, redefining business casual for the team.

As they walked to the parking lot, Chad shared a little of his story. "After interviewing with half a dozen companies, I just felt I could grow the most here. I wanted to lead, and it was as if they had a sign hanging over the front door that said, 'Leaders Made Here.' That's what clinched the deal for me."

Hearing this, the team looked at each other all thinking the same thing: *He is one of the people we just talked about!*

"Do you feel the company delivered on its promise?" Blake asked.

"Absolutely! Coming here is a decision I've never regretted," Chad said.

"Well, I hoped you would say yes, or we'd be headed back to the airport," Gary said only half in jest.

The drive to the headquarters was short but long enough for each of the group members to share highlights from their own leadership journey.

They walked into the offices and found an environment that reflected their host or vice versa. It was clean and comfortable—but *very* casual. As they walked through the offices, Kim thought she saw a dog under someone's desk. Just as she was about to ask, Chad interrupted her thought.

"Yes, you did see a dog under that desk. Well-behaved dogs are welcome!"

Gary's facial expression revealed his disbelief. He had never been anywhere like this before. Kim and

Blake didn't seem to be as taken aback by the canine co-worker.

Blake said, "I know what you two are thinking, and no, I don't think we can bring our dogs to work."

"That's probably a good thing," Gary said.

The group made their way out onto a patio. "Let's meet out here," Chad said. "It's such a beautiful day. I can't stand the thought of being inside."

Everyone took a seat and a moment to acknowledge the splendor of the day. Chad broke the silence. "How can I help you today?"

Blake said, "As you know, we want to create a leadership culture, and based on our research, you have figured it out. We're here to learn all we can."

"You are very kind. I wouldn't say we have figured it out, but we have learned a lot over the last twenty years. We have learned a few things that work in our industry and our culture, and we have learned some things that do not work."

"Let's start with some of the things that have worked," Kim said.

"Then we want to hear some of the things that haven't worked," added Gary.

Before Chad could respond, Blake chimed in by saying, "And, I would like to know why: why do you think the things that worked, worked, and why do you think the things that didn't work, didn't?"

"That's a mouthful!" Chad laughed.

"Please don't ask me to say it again,"
Blake smiled.

"I think I know what you mean. We have done so
many different things to create the culture you see here
today. We hold our strategies tightly and our tactics
loosely. Virtually everything has a season, and during
that time, we are constantly evaluating and tweaking—
both programs and our processes. Sometimes we stop
doing one thing and start doing another."

We hold our strategies tightly and our tactics loosely.

"Give us an example of something you have
stopped doing," Kim said.

"Well, let me think. . . . Here's an easy one: we
stopped requiring all our leadership training to be
done face-to-face. I know that may seem to be a
blinding flash of the obvious, but for us, it was a *huge*
shift. We are a face-to-face, highly relational culture.
Encouraging people to be trained via e-learning,
webinars, and simulcasts was a big deal.

"That decision has helped with speed and reach
and also reduced our cost significantly. It's a simple
thing, and some companies have been doing it for
many years. We were late adopters, but we've had tremendous results."

"Sounds simple enough," said Gary.

"So your training model is decentralized?" Blake asked.

"Not really—nor is it centralized. It's a hybrid. Some of it originates here and some in the field. And, we still offer many courses live, both here and in the field. We now just have more options. We've become very comfortable with this multifaceted approach."

Kim had a follow-up question ready, "Okay, that was helpful. Can you tell us something you've always done?"

Without hesitation, Chad said, "That's easy—our mentoring program."

"What can you tell us about it?" Blake asked.

"We believe leaders can learn a lot from technology and classes, but there is no substitute for what can be learned from other leaders. Every leader is trained on how to be an effective mentor. Every leader is also encouraged to be a mentor and to have a mentor. We have been doing this for decades. I will be shocked if we ever stop our emphasis on mentoring."

"Is it a formal program?" Gary was curious. He had never had a real mentor.

"The training is required for all leaders but beyond that it is not a structured or required program."

"Do you know about how many of your leaders are mentoring someone?"

"Eighty-four percent as of year-end," Chad said.

"That sounds really high for an 'informal, unstructured program,'" Kim said.

"Don't fall into the trap of thinking something has to be required to be part of your culture," Chad responded. "Mentoring is certainly part of our culture."

The next two hours were very helpful. Chad shared a lot of war stories. He talked about his experience with funding issues, senior leader involvement, return on investment, staffing, and more.

Blake knew their time was almost up. He said, "Chad, I have a final question for you. What has been the single-most important thing you have done to accelerate the growth of your leaders?"

"We don't think leadership development is driven by any *single* factor—there are many things that are important. We've talked about most of them today. However, I think your question is still valid because all factors are not created equally. Some have had greater impact than others. I would say the one that has helped our leaders the most is what we call 'The Opportunity.'"

Gary stopped taking notes and looked at Chad. "Can you tell us a little more?"

"In the early days, we thought the big deal was training—and we still think it is hugely important. But we realized training alone rarely accelerated the growth of a leader. What made it real, and made the training come alive, was the actual opportunity to lead.

"One of the questions we asked our leaders early on was 'What are the things that have helped you grow the most as a leader?' Many did mention training experiences of one sort or another, and some referenced books, classes, mentors, et cetera. But the vast majority said their *greatest learning* came as a result of *actually leading something*—The Opportunity."

"So what did you do with that insight?" Kim asked.

"We work to give emerging leaders ample opportunities to lead—as early as possible in their career."

"That's it?" Kim expected a more complicated answer.

"That's it—but don't be deceived by the simplicity of it. We found it very hard to do."

"Why?" Blake asked.

"We discovered that for most people—leaders included—the natural tendency is to avoid risk. So, when a new project would come along, the leader responsible would assign a seasoned leader regardless of the opportunity—a turnaround assignment, a new product team, a start-up venture, a merger or acquisition. It did not matter what was needed; our existing leaders rarely gave an emerging or inexperienced leader a shot. This did nothing to help young leaders grow and develop in a real-world setting."

"That is exactly the type thing our emerging leaders need, too—real-world experience," Kim said.

"We all do," Chad said. "But let me be clear: This does not mean we *always* give the next opportunity to the emerging leader. Sometimes, the seasoned leader is the right choice. However, because we recognize the power of The Opportunity, we are consciously working to provide it more often. As a result, we have many young leaders doing significant work that their counterparts at other companies won't have the chance to do for a decade or more."

"That explains why you're the number 2 guy in a multibillion-dollar business at such a young age."

"You are partially correct, but opportunity is not everything. In isolation, it is rarely enough, but as part of a larger plan, it makes a big difference."

"Thanks again for sharing your time and your story, "Blake said. "It is easy to see why your company is successful. Please let us know when you are in our town. We would love to show you around our place."

"Can I bring my dog?" Chad asked with a big grin.

"Only if he stays in the car," Gary responded.

As the team said their good-byes, Kim whispered to Chad, "Bring the dog; he can stay in my office."

⚒ Let's Review

As the team assembled for their regularly scheduled meeting, Blake joined them for the first agenda item— the debrief from his visit with Kim and Gary.

Charles was glad Blake had joined them so he could thank him publicly. He also thought it might be a good time to share a little more of his story.

"You guys may not realize what an amazing company you are creating. I am guessing few CEOs would give a day to cover for a consultant to spend a day with his family. This is a testimony to how much Blake values people and how much he believes in creating a leadership culture. His willingness to personally make a benchmarking trip rather than just ask us to do it for him sends a strong signal to the entire organization. Blake, thank you again."

Charles took a deep breath and continued. "The time with my family means more to me than you know. When we first met, I told you I was in recovery. . . ."

"How's that going?" Rose asked.

"Great. Thanks for asking." Charles hesitated and then said, "What I didn't tell you on that first day is that my wife died a few months ago, and because of my addiction and my rehab program, my daughter, Samantha, has been living with my parents. She's four years old."

Kim, in shock from Charles's revelation said, "Your wife died?"

"Yes, and losing her combined with not seeing Sam very much made the day last week with her even more valuable to me."

"Why didn't you tell us about your wife in the first meeting?" Rose asked.

"I was scared you would feel sorry for me, maybe more than you already did. The alcohol thing seemed like enough; that's all I was ready to share."

"Why now?" Gary asked.

"It didn't take long for me to trust you guys. I can see your hearts—the way you work with each other. You really do care. I guess I really need some of that care to come my way." He offered a faint smile. "It's been really hard," Charles confessed.

"Where is your daughter now?" Gary asked.

"Back with my folks."

"When will you see her again?" Kim asked.

"I'm not sure, but soon, I hope. My plan is for us to rebuild our lives together. I just have a few details and a few more issues to resolve."

"Thanks for sharing this with us. We will help any way we can," Bob added.

"I appreciate that. For now, let's create a leadership culture." Charles shifted the team's attention to their agenda. "Today, let's see what we learned in our visits. Because Blake can only be with us for the beginning of our meeting, we'll start with your visit with Chad."

Gary looked around the table and said, "I think I have been 'voluntold' to represent our group. Guys, jump in if you have anything to add.

"We met with Chad Freeman, head of Operations for a very successful company, and leadership development is a real priority for them. The promise of personal growth enticed Chad to join the company over a decade ago.

"I came up with hundreds of ideas based on this visit," he said, smiling, "but for today, I have three big takeaways."

The balance of the group breathed a collective sigh of relief. "Three ideas will be good," Charles said. "However, please don't lose your notes—we may need every one of your ideas in the months and years to come."

"Here you go," Gary began.

"One, mentoring matters. They've done this for over twenty years. Chad believes mentoring will always be part of their culture. Two, all training doesn't have to be face-to-face. They are using distance learning and computer-assisted learning. This is relatively new for them, but Chad appeared excited about the results thus far.

"And finally, giving people the chance to lead early in their career seems to have been a game changer for them. They call this 'The Opportunity.'"

As Gary was speaking, Charles had stepped to the board and wrote:

Themes

- Mentoring matters
- Multiple learning formats
- The Opportunity accelerates growth

"How did I do, guys? Does that capture the big ideas?" Gary asked.

Blake said, "I agree. Thanks for stating our findings so succinctly."

Kim nodded in agreement.

"Okay, before we expand on this list by looking at the other visit, Blake, do you have anything to add?" Charles asked.

"Just one thought. As Chad was telling us his story, he used a phrase I can't get out of my head. For him, it seemed to be a passing thought—for me, it could be a real insight."

Blake had the entire team's attention; even Bob and Kim had no idea what Blake was about to share.

"When Chad was looking for a job a decade ago, he said it was as if his company had a sign out front that said 'Leaders Made Here.' I think that is the real test of a leadership culture. What will it take for us to say with full integrity, 'Leaders Made Here'?

What will it take for us to say with full integrity, "Leaders Made Here"?

"Can you imagine the competitive advantage we would enjoy?" Blake paused and looked around the room. "That should be our mantra and our promise: Leaders Made Here. Can you guys help us make that a reality? Can we learn how to do it consistently well?"

"That is a powerful idea," Bob said.

"I would sign up for that," Kim added.

"Blake, thanks for giving us language for our challenge. We'll figure out how to make that promise a reality," Charles said.

"That's all I have to add. Thanks for letting me join you on the visit." As he moved toward the door, he added, "Sorry, I've got to go now. I look forward to meeting with you again. Please call me if you need anything."

"Thanks again for the gift of time with my family."

"Glad to do it. See you guys again soon."

As soon as Blake left, the team turned their conversation to what they had just heard.

"Leaders Made Here. I like the simplicity of it," Gary said. "I like the promise," Rose added.

"Yes, but how do we do it?" Charles interjected. "That's what we are trying to learn. Bob, I want to turn the floor over to you to share our findings from our first visit."

"In keeping with the format Gary established, I'll not share all our observations, just the key themes. I think there were three, with some overlap with what you experienced," he said looking at Charles and Kim.

Bob proceeded to talk about the three themes. As before, Charles added them to their running list of observations. Bob described the training programs, leadership support, and the importance of a common definition of leadership.

Themes

- Mentoring matters
- Multiple learning formats
- The Opportunity accelerates growth
- Lots of formal training programs
- Senior-level support critical
- Common definition was huge

"I think this is great!" Charles said. "It looks to me like we are right on track."

"I agree," Rose said.

"Help me," Bob said. "How are we 'right on track'?"

"I think I see it, too," Kim chimed in.

"Thanks," Bob said sarcastically. "Make me feel like a laggard."

"No, really. I can already see some of these best practices in play in our organization. And, where there are gaps, we need to know that. I don't consider that a failure—I see it as a step toward success. A problem well-defined is half-solved."

"So you're telling me the glass is half-full, not half-empty?" Bob asked.

"No, I'm telling you the glass is completely full—half water and half air." Rose gave Bob a playful smile.

"Now that is optimism."

"No, I prefer to think of it as realism," Rose said.

It Just Happens

The team's progress was encouraging. The benchmarking trips were yielding both validation for some
of what the organization was already doing and ideas
for future enhancements. And, although some of the
internal interviews had proven challenging, overall they
had been productive. The final stakeholder interview
was now scheduled; Gary would meet with Amanda to
get the CFO's perspective on leadership development.

Gary showed up early with his questions in hand.
He had also talked to the other team members who
had conducted similar sessions. He was ready—
he hoped.

Gary anxiously stepped into Amanda's office.
"Thanks for agreeing to meet with me. As you probably know, our team is trying to determine how we
might strengthen our organization. I'm here to get
your perspective."

"Yes, thanks for coming by. Tell me again, what are
we calling this?"

"What are you referring to, ma'am?"

"The project, the program—what is it you have
been charged to do, exactly?"

"Well, the project doesn't have an official name. However, what we are trying to do is help build a leadership culture."

"Yes, yes, that's it. That's what worries me."

"Which part?"

"This whole thing seems weird to me."

"Why?" Gary asked.

"'Leadership culture' seems like a fancy way to say people should do their jobs."

"Say more about that." Gary had no idea what Amanda was trying to say.

"If an organization is well led, it just works. It's like electricity. I don't know how it works—it just does. People are empowered to do their jobs. It just happens. I don't know how else to explain it," Amanda mused.

"That is exactly why we are doing this work," Gary responded. "To ensure it *always* works. No organization drifts to greatness. And besides, your 'it just happens' theory might be true in a small, uncomplicated organization. I'm guessing that's exactly how it felt when you joined the company. How many employees were here when you started?"

"About twenty."

"Really?" He was shocked. "Today, we have thousands!"

"Yes, and we've always had enough leaders."

"Where do they come from?" Gary probed.

"I don't know; they just show up," Amanda said.

"Oh, yeah—like electricity. That sounds risky to me. Besides, I think our 'it just happens' and 'they just show up' plan is starting to fail us. We have open leadership positions *today*—in your area of the business."

Amanda did not have a ready response.

Gary continued, "When we were small, immersion and osmosis proved to be an adequate means of filling our leadership needs. You and your contemporaries learned a lot about leadership by just paying attention. It was really more of an apprentice model. Unfortunately, we have outgrown that approach."

"You may be right. I just do not like it."

■ ■ ■

The team's next visit would be different. Whereas the previous visits had been to a financial service company and a high-tech company, this next organization was in the service business. They were big but not as big as the other two and domestic, not international. They were only slightly bigger than the team's own company.

Upon arrival, Rose, Bob, and Charles immediately noticed the environment—the place was professional, yet casual and comfortable. You might think the two other companies the team had visited had morphed into one.

Their host for the day was Tom Buchanan, the chief learning officer and a member of the company's senior leadership team.

After some introductory comments by everyone, Tom asked the same question their other hosts had asked: "How can I help you today?"

Charles began by asking, "What is the most valuable thing you have done to grow your organization's leadership?

"Well, Charles," Tom began, "we decided a long time ago we needed a scorecard."

"A leadership scorecard?" Rose asked.

"Yes. Nothing improves without measurement, and leadership is no exception."

Nothing improves without measurement, and leadership is no exception.

"How hard was it to find the right metric?" Bob asked.

"We couldn't. Believe me, we tried. We finally abandoned the idea of a single metric. We know organizations that have only one measure of leadership effectiveness, and it seems to work for them. But we could not quite figure it out. So we have a scorecard that contains several key metrics."

"And those are. . . ." Rose had her pen in hand.

"I am not sure I want to tell you," Tom smiled. "I have a strong sense that what makes our scorecard work for us is the fact we created it for us—for our business, with our goals and objectives in mind. My fear is that to share ours might bias you as you decide what matters in your organization. Also, a critical part of the process is senior leadership input. You do not want to miss that."

Bob spoke up and said, "This feels a little like the kid who asked his mom how to spell something and she tells him to look it up. The kid's response: 'How can I look it up if I don't know how to spell it?'"

"Fair enough," Tom conceded. "Let's do this. We will have a short working session on scorecards. I'll facilitate." Tom walked over to a flipchart that was in the corner of the conference room.

Tom began, "Let's start with what a scorecard is designed to do." He wrote on the flipchart as he talked.

"A scorecard should answer at least four questions: 'What's most important now?' 'Is our performance improving or declining?' 'What impact are our interventions having?' And, 'Are we winning?'"

When he finished speaking, he stepped back to reveal what he had written on the flipchart:

Why have a scorecard?

- Clarifies what's important now
- Shows our performance trend
- Tracks the impact of our interventions
- Allows us to see actual performance vs. our goals

He continued, "So, what are the most important things you are working to accomplish in leadership development at this point?"

"That's one of the issues we need to get clarity around," Charles said.

"I would suggest you figure that out first. Then ask, what are the most critical tasks and results you want to focus on? Keep the list short; four to five items will be plenty."

"I understand the importance of figuring this out for ourselves," Rose said. "And, I understand why you don't want to give us the answer. However, I would love to know some of the things you and your team *considered* when creating your scorecard."

"You tell me—what do you think we considered?" Tom said again with a big smile. He obviously was not going to give out answers easily.

Rose said, "I am guessing you had metrics around 'reach'—things like the number of leaders attending your programs."

"You are correct, but reach defined broadly. Reach can include training we deliver, training we sponsor, training we recommend, technology-based training, mentoring relationships that we facilitate, and so forth."

"Is reach really just a numbers game?" Bob asked in a tone that betrayed his skepticism.

"Yes and no," Tom said. "One benefit of reach metrics is they allow you to know how many of your current and emerging leaders speak your leadership language. Therefore, we want that number to be 100 percent. That's why reach matters to us."

"Did you have any metrics in consideration that focused on results?" Charles asked.

"Yes—we had a huge debate around this one. We all know that when performance is an issue, lack of training is rarely the root cause of the problem. However, we do find that training is always part of superior performance—people must have the knowledge and skills to do their work."

Tom continued, "I'm sensing you accept the challenge and the significance of creating your own scorecard. I will offer two more thoughts, and we can move on.

"One, think beyond traditional learning metrics. If you invest the time and seek input from key senior leaders, your leadership scorecard can be a very powerful tool."

"Can you give us a couple of examples?" Rose asked.

"Leadership diversity, retention, ready-now leaders, and inside versus outside selections, to name a few," Tom said.

"Thanks, that's helpful," Bob said.

"My final scorecard thought for today: You can, and should, change your key metrics as the needs of the organization change. Do not get locked in, or *you* will become irrelevant to your business."

"Can you say a little more about irrelevance?" Rose asked.

"If you are answering questions no one is asking or solving problems that don't really matter, you will be viewed as irrelevant," Tom responded.

Bob said, "Today has been really helpful. It sounds like the scorecard may have been the most important element in building a leadership culture."

"Actually, no—it is not. First, there is *no single-most important thing* because no single thing will suffice. It will take many elements carefully orchestrated to build the type of culture I imagine you and your team have envisioned."

Tom continued, "There is no one thing that will make it happen." He paused and then said, "However, *there is one thing that will make it impossible.*"

"You certainly have our attention now,"
Rose said.

"Please continue," Charles said.

"The one thing that can prevent you from creating
a leadership culture is leadership."

"Is this a riddle?" Bob asked.

"No, I'm serious," Tom said.

"You mean leadership has to support the effort?
Fund it, talk it up, and teach classes?"

"All the things you mentioned are really good
things for leaders to do, but there is one thing that
supersedes all you mentioned: leaders must walk the
talk. In your organization, you teach servant leadership, correct?" Tom asked.

"Yes, we do; we believe all great leaders are ser-
vants first," Rose said.

"Fine, but if you say that and your leaders do not
serve, then your leadership culture is dead in the
water. People always watch the leader. They are looking for at least two things, first and foremost: clues
as to what's really important, and they're also trying
to determine if they can trust the leader," Tom said.
"And, they often link these two. They watch to see if
the leader's behaviors match his or her words.

"As strange as it may sound, the number one reason most companies do not have a leadership culture
is their current leadership."

The number one reason most companies do not have a leadership culture is their current leadership.

"Got it," Charles nodded.

He was thankful Blake had always encouraged and modeled servant leadership. The question on Charles's mind was different: could they help *all their leaders* become servant leaders?

Just Do It

The team was excited about all they were learning. They were even more excited about the pragmatic nature of the themes—it all seemed doable to them. As they approached the final visit, they were eager to test some of what they had learned thus far. Due to travel logistics and expenses for a trip to Europe, not to mention perceptions, Gary scheduled a video-conference with Hans Kline, the head of leadership development for a smaller, wildly successful, global organization with a strong reputation.

"Good afternoon! Thanks for agreeing to meet with us," Gary said.

"I'm delighted," Hans said.

After the group exchanged introductions and brief work histories, Charles went to the agenda. "Hans, there are several things we want to talk to you about today. As you know from our initial call several months ago, we are attempting to do what you have already done—we want to create a leadership culture. We've done a lot of work since then and reached a few conclusions. One of our goals for today is to get your reaction to our work thus far."

The team gave Hans an update on their process and progress. Charles then asked Rose to share an overview of their previous visits.

Hans listened intently. Then he said, "I think I understand. I have a few questions for you. Where are you today relative to this work? How many of the desired activities are actually taking place already?"

"Great questions," Charles said. "We're not even sure what the desired behaviors are at this point."

"Okay, that's fair. Would everyone agree on your current effectiveness as it relates to developing leaders?"

"Probably not." Kim said.

"Then you will want to establish an internal benchmark for your key leaders specifically—they need to acknowledge where you are today. This may provide confidence, or urgency, or both." Hans said.

"How would you suggest we do that?" Bob asked.

"Perhaps you should consider an assessment."

"An assessment?" Rose asked.

"Yes, before I begin any journey, I have always found it helpful to confirm my starting point. It tends to clarify one's options. Without clarity on where you are, you could be making great time—but in the wrong direction."

"Thanks, Hans. This is very helpful. We have an intuitive sense of where we are but nothing as complete or as definitive as what you're suggesting."

"I have one more question," Bob said. "I know our time is almost up. What should we call what we're doing?"

"Nothing."

"Excuse me," Rose said. She didn't know if they lost the signal for a moment. "Did you say 'nothing'?"

Without clarity on where you are, you could be making great time— but in the wrong direction.

"Yes—don't call it anything. Just establish clear goals, a sound strategy, agree on the necessary tactics, and execute them well. This is not a campaign; it is not an event; it is not the flavor of the month. You want this to become the new normal.

"Let me help you. I have studied your company, also." Hans flashed a wry smile. "Based on your retention rates, I am assuming you are very good at selecting people."

"Thank you, Hans," Bob said. "We think selecting the right people really matters."

"What do you call it?" Hans asked.

"Call what?" Gary was confused.

"Your selection process," Hans said.

"We don't have a name for it," Rose said.

"Why not?"

"Because it is just what we do, who we are, and what we believe."

"So I suggest you apply the same logic to your plans for building a leadership culture. Do not name it—just do it.

"However, there is one thing I would think you should be very clear about. Not only clear—you should be in perfect unison on this one."

"What's that?" Bob asked.

"Why—why the work you're proposing is critically important to your organization. Let's go back to your people selection process. Why do you exercise such great care in selecting people?"

"Because people decisions are the most important decisions a leader makes," Kim said.

"Look at what just happened!" Hans insisted with energy in his voice. "I was watching. Kim, the most junior person on your team, gave me your answer, and all of you nodded in agreement. You all know *why* you place such a high priority on selecting the right people—it's become part of your DNA as an organization. You will ultimately need that same level of clarity throughout your organization regarding *why* you place a priority on building a leadership culture.

"You do not need to call it anything, but you do need complete unity on why it is mission-critical for your organization."

With that comment, Hans looked at his watch and said, "Sorry, my time is almost up. I would love to hear about your progress and your success in the months to come. Please contact me again if I can help."

"Good-bye. Thank you so much!" Charles said quickly, as the videoconference ended.

"That was really good," Bob said.

"We need to decide what to do with the ideas Hans just shared with us. Can we take a short break and then reconvene for our debrief?" Gary asked.

"I have a better idea," Charles suggested. "There is a coffee shop around the corner and I'm buying. Let's meet there."

Judging by the team's reaction, this was an outstanding idea.

■ ■ ■

After they picked up their drinks, the group moved to a table in the corner.

"Charles, can you actually have a meeting without a whiteboard or a flipchart?" Gary poked.

Everyone laughed, even Charles. "It will be hard, but I'll try.

"What did we hear?" Charles went quickly into facilitator mode, even without a flipchart.

"Hans seemed to really understand our challenge," Kim said.

"What about his line of questioning about where we are today?" Charles asked.

"I thought he made a good point. We can probably create more urgency if we have some data," Kim said.

"Let's do as he suggested," Bob said. "Let's create an assessment. We can use our findings when we make our presentation to the senior team."

"I like it. Should we work on that today?" Rose asked.

"No, let me work on it and get back to the team," Bob volunteered.

"I'll help. I have a couple of ideas already," Gary said.

"We will need to move quickly. We should create the framework and conduct the assessment in the next week or two. That will give us a few days to prepare our final presentation."

"Any final thoughts before we adjourn?" "Yes," Rose said. "I want to have one more meeting with David."

"You do?" Bob said. "Why?"

"A couple of reasons. He is a senior leader whose opinion matters. And he's the biggest skeptic we know about to date. Who knows, maybe I can learn something that will help us prepare our presentation."

"Do you want someone to go with you?" Charles asked.

"No, I will be fine. Remember, we are all on the same team," Rose smiled.

Never Too Late

Rose contacted David's assistant and asked for a fifteen-minute meeting. Remembering her first encounter, she told the assistant no chairs were required.

David greeted Rose and apologized for his behavior in their previous meeting. "Thanks for giving me a second chance. Please have a seat." This was not the welcome Rose had expected, but she was relieved.

"Well, thank you for agreeing to another meeting. As I thought about our last meeting, obviously, I was not on my best behavior, either. Let's start over."

"Sounds like a fine idea," David said.

Rose spent the next few minutes giving David a quick overview of what the team had been doing and what she believed were some of the ideas that might serve their company in the future.

"We just might be able to pull this off," David said.

Rose tried to hide her amazement. "Thanks for the endorsement?" she said quizzically.

"Well, I must admit, I've had my doubts about the whole thing ever since Blake told us about the work, even before he hired Charles. I had huge reservations.

I guess that is what I was trying to communicate in our first visit."

"You were *very* clear in our last visit; I knew you had major reservations," Rose affirmed with a grimace. "And, I appreciated your candor. But I must ask, what changed your mind?"

"First, I want to say, I think it is going to be much more difficult than any of you may believe."

"Why?" Rose asked.

"If you guys think I am the only skeptic in the company, you are kidding yourselves. I am guessing you will find hundreds of us. Many, like me, learned leadership on our own. We didn't have training, or mentoring, or metrics, or any of the things we've been talking about. Just trial and error, hard work, and for those of us who survived, probably a measure of good luck."

If you guys think I am the only skeptic in the company, you are kidding yourselves.

"Let me ask again, what changed your mind? What changed since our last meeting?" Rose persisted.

"Your first visit was not a waste of your time. When you confronted me with the fact I did not have enough leaders, you had me. After you left, I began to think about the 'process' for developing leaders and my own leadership journey. . . ."

David stopped as if he wasn't sure he wanted to continue. Then he said, "I realized how bad a leader I was early in my career. Hell, I'm not that great today. But I have learned some things. I'm not as lousy as I used to be."

He paused again. "This is hard to say, but I could have done better. In our first meeting after the accident, when Blake said the cause was really 'leadership error,' he was talking to me!"

"Hold on—I wasn't there, but I think he was talking about *every* leader in the company," Rose said.

"Maybe. But he could have been talking just to me. I could have served my team and our company better. If I had, maybe those men and women would still be alive today. If someone like you, or Charles, had been around to help me. . . ." He looked like he was about to cry.

"I regret not leading better. Your work should give future leaders in our company no excuses and no regrets concerning poor leadership. Future leaders can leave a better legacy than I have. Our leaders and our company should thrive because of the work you are doing. I am proud to support your efforts!"

Rose didn't know what to say. After an awkward moment, she said, "Thank you for your transparency. It's never too late—your story and your legacy are still being written."

Connect the Dots

Charles knew the next phase of the project was the most critical. All the team had been trying to do thus far was find the truth regarding how to build a leadership culture. Now, they would attempt to translate what they had learned into something culturally relevant for their organization. They needed to create a strategy they could execute.

At the team's next meeting, after their usual join-up time, Charles went to the whiteboard and asked, "What's happened since our last meeting?"

"Well, I had an interview with Amanda," Gary said.

"How did that go?" Bob asked.

"Let's just say, David is not the only skeptic in senior leadership. Besides that, she offered a few tactical suggestions. I will share those at the appropriate time."

"What is her primary concern?" Charles asked.

"Well, it's hard to articulate. Amanda seems to prefer an approach to leadership development I would call 'spontaneous combustion.' She said more than once, 'it just happens' and 'leaders just show up.' She described it like electricity—she doesn't know how it works—it just does. She seems to be willing to leave the filling of leadership positions totally to chance."

"I have seen similar attitudes in other organizations," Charles said. "It is what I call the 'waiting on Superman' syndrome. The hope is when you find yourself in a dire situation, a superhero, a.k.a. a leader, will miraculously appear. The core problem with this approach is that hope is not a strategy." Blake had imparted this nugget of wisdom from his visit with Jack.

"We'll just have to show Amanda that a more systematic approach will generate better results. Don't worry; we will find a way to serve Amanda and her team. We'll win her over."

"Maybe. I hope so," Gary said.

Charles said, "A final thought on this. When we encounter resistance—and we will continue to do so—remember, we are all on the same team. Now, how about our third field visit? Insights?"

As Bob pulled out his notes, Rose said, "I don't have as many notes as Bob, but I can tell you what I learned."

"Okay, let's hear it," Charles said.

"We are going to need a leadership scorecard."

"Really? That sounds hard," Kim said.

"It can be," Charles said, "but we'll create it in partnership with senior leaders. It will be a great tool to assess our gaps and our progress."

"Anything else?" Charles directed his question to Bob who was flipping through pages and pages of notes. The team waited.

"Yes," Bob said finally. "Tom's final challenge to us was about the one thing that can derail all our efforts to create a leadership culture."

"And that would be . . . ?" Kim asked impatiently.

"Leadership," Bob said.

"Leadership?" Gary didn't understand.

"Yes," Charles said. "Tom reminded us that people always watch the leaders. If we are not walking the talk, we will undermine all we are trying to accomplish."

People always watch the leaders.

"That's heavy," Kim said.

"Yes and no," Charles continued. "Leaders understand this responsibility and carry the load willingly. Those who cannot shoulder the weight of leadership, or do not want to, don't lead—or at least not for long. Anything else from your visit?"

"Pages of notes we can save for later—more tactical conversations," Bob said.

"And finally, there was Hans," Charles said. "I think he helped us most with how to sell our ideas internally."

"Right. The assessment is a huge part of that," Kim said.

"And, he challenged us not to call this anything," Rose added.

"So, where are we? Let's go back and look at the big picture. What are the themes we have noticed throughout the process thus far?"

"I'm glad you mentioned that," said Kim. "I've noticed many of the same ideas surfacing in each visit. Why do you think that is?"

"Maybe it is because all the companies we selected have already created a leadership culture. And, maybe—this is just an educated guess, but maybe, there is a common path others have already discovered," Gary said.

"That is our premise," Charles said. "Let's recap all the big ideas from our work thus far and see what we can unearth."

After an extended period of time combing through their notes from the visits and the internal interviews, the team had compiled the following list:

Themes

- Mentoring matters
- Multiple learning formats and opportunities
- "The Opportunity" accelerates growth
- Lots of formal training programs
- Senior-level support is critical
- Common definition is huge
- Metrics matter
- Leaders must walk the talk
- Outstanding facilities
- Pet-friendly
- Technology-enabled training
- Leadership development can be a recruiting tool

Gary broke the silence. "What should we do next?"

"I think we can tighten the list," Bob said. "Some of these items don't pass my filter for 'themes.'"

"Okay," Rose said reluctantly. "I guess we can scratch the 'pet-friendly' comment."

"And I think we can move past the idea of outstanding facilities," Charles said. "We did see one amazing campus, but the others created the culture we are looking for with modest facilities."

"Leadership as a recruiting tool is a big idea, but it seems like an outcome, not an input, so let's take it off the list." The group indicated their general agreement with Gary on this point.

"Can we combine any of the remaining items?" Charles wondered out loud.

"Maybe," Rose said. "'Classroom,' 'technology-enabled training,' and 'mentoring' seem to all be about delivery mechanisms for content."

"Or instruction," Kim said.

"Let's see if bundling them and representing the idea with the words 'Varied instructional methods' will work," Charles said as a facilitator trying to move a group to closure.

After a few other tweaks, Charles said, "So our new list would read . . . ," as he turned the page on the flipchart and wrote:

To Create a Leadership Culture, We Need . . .

- Varied instructional methods
- Agreement on what leadership means
- The power of "The Opportunity"
- Metrics to matter
- Leaders to walk the talk

"Is that the strategy?" Gary asked.

"Perhaps," Charles said as he looked at the list. "It's not very sticky."

"Sticky?" Bob said.

"Memorable, catchy. There's no hook. It's just a list of big ideas," Charles added.

"It may not be sticky, but I don't think it's in the right order, either," Bob said.

"Should there be an order?" Rose asked.

"Let's think about it. There is probably a logic, if not a sequence," Charles said thoughtfully. "It is supposed to be our blueprint for building a leadership culture."

"Yeah, if we like Leaders Made Here, aren't we trying to inform our process for delivering on that promise?" Kim asked.

"I guess you could think of it like that," Gary agreed.

"Well, if you are going to make something or build something like a house, you start with the foundation, right?" Rose asked the group.

"I guess so," Gary said tentatively.

"Okay, which of these items represents the foundation?" Charles asked.

"Agreement on what leadership means," Rose said.

Charles wrote the number *1* by it on the flipchart.

"What would be a logical second step?" Charles was pushing the group a little.

"Training. Once people know what leadership is, they need the knowledge and ability to do it," Kim asserted.

"And then you would want to provide the opportunity. That is what we heard on our visit—the opportunity accelerates leadership development," Bob said, thinking that made sense.

"Okay—we have the first three. Which would be next?"

"I guess you would want to measure the success of what you are doing. Put the metrics as number 4," Rose said.

"Then by default, the 'walk the talk' one is last." Charles finished the numbering process.

"But 'last' may not be the best way to think about it if it is essential to our success," Bob said.

"I think they are all essential," Kim added.

"Agreed," Charles said as he wrote out the list again and this time he changed the heading.

To Create a Leadership Culture . . .

- Agreement on what leadership means
- Varied instructional methods
- The power of "The Opportunity"
- Metrics matter
- Leaders must walk the talk

"That seems like a strong list to me," Kim said.

"How can we say it better? The structure is not right. We need to put it in an action tense. What is it we are going to *do*?"

"I think the first one could be 'Define it,'" Gary offered.

"What's the 'it'?"

"Leadership," Gary said. "That seems like the most logical starting point. And it was the big idea from your first visit. There must be agreement on what you mean when you say leadership before you can build a culture around it."

"That's good. If the first one is 'Define it,' the second could be 'Teach it,'" Bob said.

"And what would we teach?" Charles asked.

Rose was the first to comment. "Our leadership point of view, our definition, the skills and competencies needed to lead well."

"This seems to be working. Let's stay with the 'it' theme," Charles encouraged.

"What's next?"

"I don't know about the opportunity one," Kim admitted, "but the fourth one could be 'Measure it.'"

"Okay. Anything else?" Gary asked.

"I think the last one is . . . ," Bob began, but Rose cut him off.

"No, wait. Let me guess. 'Finish it'? 'Execute it'? 'Book it'? 'Slam it'? 'Conquer it'? 'Repeat it'? I know it has to end with 'it.'"

"No, no, no, no, no, and no—although 'Repeat it' is a pretty good idea," Bob said.

"I give up. What is it?"

Before Bob could answer, Kim said, "Model it!"

"That's what I was thinking," Bob said. "Leaders must model the attitude, commitment, and leadership behaviors they are advocating for others."

"People always want to know if you're smoking what you're selling," Rose said.

"What?" Charles asked.

"Just something I've heard other people say." Rose blushed.

"Okay, all we need is some way to represent the idea of The Opportunity," Charles said.

"And it has to end in 'it,'" Rose reminded the group with a grin.

"What do you propose?" Charles asked. "How about 'Do it'?"

"Sounds like a failed attempt at a sneaker ad."

"Okay, how about 'Try it.'"

"Sounds like an old TV commercial—'Try it, you'll like it.'"

"Maybe," Bob said. "Or, how about 'Apply it'?"

No response from the group.

"Other options?" Charles asked.

"'Give it'—as in give the opportunity to lead?" Gary's tone reflected uncertainty.

"What is it we really want emerging leaders to do with their newfound knowledge and skills?" Charles asked.

"Practice it," Bob said. "It's the practice that cements and accelerates the learning."

"True," Kim said.

"I like it," Gary added.

"Me, too," Rose agreed.

Charles wrote it in and the entire team stopped to study what could be their newfound strategy.

To Create a Leadership Culture...

- Define it
- Teach it
- Practice it
- Measure it
- Model it

"Could it be that simple?" Rose asked.

"Deceivingly simple," Charles said. "We have done a good job stating it succinctly, but it will require a lot of work to move from paper to practice. That will be our next challenge: how do we turn this plan into reality?"

The Pitch

The next day, Charles was up early again. Based on his newfound commitment to run, he headed for the streets. As he ran, he thought about all that had transpired in the previous few years. He had both regrets and blessings to reflect upon. One of the blessings was the work Blake had given him.

At the weekly check-in with Blake, he was excited to share the team's progress.

"Good morning. How are you today?" Blake asked.

Charles, talking a little bit faster than usual, said, "Fantastic! I ran five miles this morning. Running has really helped me clear my mind *and* strengthen my body. How are you?"

"Really good. Anxious to see what you and the team have come up with," Blake said.

"I can't wait to share the new strategy with you. We need to know your thoughts. Did we miss anything? Do you think it will stand the test of time? What will others think and do when they hear our recommendations? What should we do next?"

"Hold on—slow down," Blake said. "One question at a time."

Charles laughed. "Okay, I've prepared a single slide to summarize our findings. We have formulated a strategy with five elements."

"Let's take a look," Blake said.

Charles handed Blake the page and said, "Five ongoing commitments. . . ."

To Create a Leadership Culture . . .

✔ **Define it**—Forge a consensus regarding our organization's working definition of leadership.

✔ **Teach it**—Ensure everyone knows our leadership point of view and leaders have the skills required to succeed.

✔ **Practice it**—Create opportunities for leaders and emerging leaders to lead; stretch assignments prove and improve leaders.

✔ **Measure it**—Track the progress of our leadership development efforts, adjusting strategies and tactics accordingly.

✔ **Model it**—Walk the talk and lead by example—people always watch the leader.

For the next twenty minutes, Charles explained to Blake what the five tenets of the strategy meant and how the team had reached these conclusions.

After he finished, Blake said, "I like it a lot! Congratulations."

"Thanks—the team has done really strong work on this," Charles said. "I love the five elements! They seem doable."

Blake added, "It makes good common sense, too."

"I know. That also worries me just a little. What we have created is not really flashy. It almost feels pedestrian in some ways."

"Hey," Blake said, "my dad always reminded me, 'Common sense is not always common.' I agree—it is not flashy. Neither is blocking and tackling for a Super Bowl winner or passing the ball for an NBA champion. It is obvious, and probably what makes it so powerful.

"Organizations capable of executing on the obvious can create real competitive advantage. Too many leaders call plays they cannot run. When they do, they lose. Our organization can do this. Effective and doable beats flashy and improbable every time. I really like it.

Organizations capable of executing on the obvious can create real competitive advantage.

"When do you plan to share this with the senior team?" Blake asked.

"You tell me. I was thinking two weeks from now at our next meeting."

"Sounds good," Blake said. "I have one more thing I'd like you to help me think about."

"And that is?" Charles asked.

"What do we call what we're doing? Should it have a name? A slogan? A battle cry? A brand? A motto? A mascot? I'm not sure. Do we call it 'Leaders Made Here'?"

"Let me start by saying, the entire team loves the idea of Leaders Made Here. We believe the value in this simple statement could help immeasurably."

"I know," Blake said. "I have been thinking about it. Leaders Made Here can provide encouragement, accountability, create competitive advantage, and is a promise to employees and candidates alike."

"Agreed. It can also help differentiate us in the war for talent—it is our promise, but we don't think it is the *name* we should give our leadership development efforts. Let's just make it the way we do business," Charles suggested.

"That makes sense. We really don't want it to become a program. Let's not call it anything at this point—let's just do it!" Blake said.

■ ■ ■

In the days leading up to the presentation, the team followed Hans's advice and created an assessment to help the organization understand the current state of their leadership development efforts. Although their plan was to survey only a portion of the employees, they were optimistic the data would help them make their case for change. And, as suspected, the survey confirmed the gaps in their current approach:

- *The majority of current leaders could not articulate the organization's point of view on leadership. (This was to be expected—the organization has never articulated a common definition of leadership.)*
- *Only a small percentage of current leaders had attended any of the leadership programs offered over the previous 24 months. Many had never attended any leadership development class or course.*
- *Of the emerging leaders surveyed, less than one-third of them were confident about the organization's approach to leadership development.*
- *Less than 10 percent of all cross-functional teams were being led by emerging leaders.*
- *An even smaller percentage of leaders were involved in any form of mentoring program within the company.*
- *And finally, only a modest number of current leaders had "high confidence" in their successor.*

These findings would be included, but not featured, in the upcoming presentation. This was no time to throw rocks at current leaders or past decisions.

However, it was a time to consider the future. These results revealed past chapters of the organization's history. The decision to be made: Did current leadership want to write a different story for the future?

■ ■ ■

On the day of the presentation, Charles showed up early. He was as prepared as he could be as he walked into the conference room.

"Thanks for the chance to be with you today," Charles smiled. "Since this is my first time to do this, I don't know what the typical presentation looks like. However, based on the agenda, it looks like I should begin with an overview of next year's plan and conclude with our budget request. I don't want to start there.

"I want to begin by asking you to think about what you want to be true twenty years from now. Some of you will have retired and may be on a beach in the tropics at that point, but several of you probably plan to still be here. And for those who will be gone, I'd invite you to think with me about what kind of organization you want to leave behind.

"What kind of company do you want to have built two decades from now? What do you want to be known for? How successful will we be as an organization? The answers to these questions and many others will be determined by the decisions you make regarding plans and budgets.

"Today, many would say this is a great company. Why? Have you given that much thought? I know the answer—leadership. You and you and you," Charles said, making eye contact with several members of the group, "and hundreds of other leaders like you have enabled us to be a strong organization. Hats off to you and your fellow leaders. My family and the families of thousands of employees are very thankful for your leadership.

"But that's past tense. Today, we have new challenges; what about the future? Can we double and triple the size and impact of this business in the next decades? Only if we raise up leaders to make it happen. Everything does rise and fall on leadership.

"That's why our plan is a long-range plan. The ideas I am about to share with you are too big to be constrained by, or executed within, an annual planning cycle.

"We don't want to just train individual leaders, although we'll continue to do that. We want to create a leadership culture. We believe leadership can become our primary competitive advantage. We want to become known as an organization that can proudly and confidently say, 'Leaders Made Here.'

"To do this we have created a strategy that contains five elements—I would ask you to think of these as five commitments. We didn't invent these ourselves; we benchmarked some of the best companies in the world. These companies represent diverse industries, and most are already larger than us. We thought that was an important part of our process. Having adequate leadership for twelve employees is one thing, but it's quite another to provide it for 100,000.

"I have prepared a packet to leave with you outlining in greater detail our new strategy. Today, we only have time for a quick overview." He went back to the board and wrote:

The Five Commitments of a Leadership Culture

- Define it
- Teach it
- Practice it
- Measure it
- Model it

Charles then offered a brief explanation of each element. When he reviewed "Measure it," he referenced the assessment results.

Charles graciously accepted all questions and comments about the validity of the assessment results. He explained this was only intended to give a glimpse of the current reality. However, he held his ground—this snapshot pointed to real gaps and opportunities.

Charles, in an attempt to end this segment of his presentation on a higher note, said, "Besides, the value of an assessment is not the assessment."

"What do you mean?" Blake asked.

"Several months ago, I received my first physical and failed miserably. I was overweight and out of shape; my cholesterol was horrible, and much more. I could have chosen numerous reactions: anger, denial, excuses, or any number of other options. The path I took was to create a positive response to the findings—new diet, new exercise patterns. I started to run, found an accountability partner, and regularly scheduled blood tests are now part of my life. The results: my latest blood work was good, I've lost ten pounds, and I'm scheduled to run my first half marathon.

"There is no real value in an assessment—true value can only be realized in our response.

There is no real value in an assessment—true value can only be realized in our response.

Charles continued, "Thanks for your thoughts on the data. I hoped this would start a good discussion. We are absolutely convinced that nothing improves without measurement. Therefore, we are committed to finding the best way to measure our progress.

"Finally, 'Model it.' For some of our leaders, this will be a huge challenge. Thankfully, we have many who get it and are already working to grow as servant leaders. This is a big deal.

"One final word of encouragement: Before you consider us finished here, please don't let this process degenerate into merely a budget exercise. If that is ultimately what drives this process, our future will be compromised. I am asking you to consider a much bigger question than 'How much will this cost?'

"You will meet every year to talk about funding; like the tide, budgets will rise and fall. However, that should be a secondary consideration. The more important question is:

"How great do you want this organization to be— and for how long?

"That is the strategic decision you can make today. If you support building a leadership culture, you will be casting a vote for a better future. You will be casting a vote to build an enduring, great organization."

Charles concluded by saying, "The team is committed to helping each leader, and our entire organization, reach our full potential. We believe a leadership culture will best position us to do just that. We all want to tell our children and grandchildren we helped build a truly great organization. And, when we recruit the next generation of leaders, we want to say with full confidence, 'Join us: **Leaders Made Here!**'"

Decision Time

When Charles left the meeting, his team was waiting for him. "How was it?" Rose asked excitedly.

"We'll have to wait and see," Charles said. "They were very good listeners. They asked thoughtful questions and I answered them. Nothing I wouldn't have expected."

"What did they say about the assessment results?" Kim asked.

"They were not happy with the numbers. They also were not sure that long-term we were asking the best questions to judge our progress toward a leadership culture. I welcomed their input and promised them a copy of our new scorecard as soon as it is completed."

"What's next?" Bob asked.

"We should go back to work. We have a lot to do regardless of how much money we have in next year's budget," Charles said.

Gary was a bit confused. "I agree with 'go back to work,' but I don't understand your last comment, 'regardless of how much money.'"

Charles responded, "Let me say it like this: We now have a picture of the future we did not have six months ago. Even if our budget were cut in half, I still want to create a leadership culture. How about you?"

"Absolutely!" Gary said and the others nodded in agreement.

"Then let's not find ourselves waiting. We have work to do. We have seen a preferred future. Let's go about the business of turning it into reality. It may take five years, ten years, who knows? Maybe you will invest your entire career bringing it to life. I hope you guys are up for the climb. I believe it will be an amazing adventure."

Charles hadn't planned it, but he had just taken his leadership to a higher level. He was not just executing what Blake wanted; he was leading the team to accomplish something bigger than themselves—something too big for any of them to do alone. As a result, the organization had just taken a step forward—and so had Charles.

■ ■ ■

As Charles was leaving the building, he ran into Blake. "What brings you to this part of the building?"

"I was coming to see you about your presentation," Blake said.

"Oh. Am I in trouble?"

"I came to say thank you. I've received three calls already about what a tremendous job you did today. Two of the members have commented specifically about your idea that leadership could someday become our primary competitive advantage. What an intriguing thought," Blake smiled. "Let's talk about the future. I want to modify your assignment."

"You do?"

"Yes, as you recall, in addition to helping us create a leadership culture, I asked you to help us find Sally's replacement."

"Yes, I remember, I have been thinking about that from day 1. I think the team is strong. Bob appears to be the one with the most near-term potential."

"Glad to hear about Bob, but I've been thinking, too. I do not want you to work on finding Sally's replacement any longer."

"Why not?"

"I want you to take the job. You can move Sam here before she starts to school. I am sure you can find a qualified nanny. My team has great respect for the way you have led this project. They have confidence in your leadership—and that is a big deal. What do you think?"

"I didn't see that coming," Charles said.

"Why not?"

"I'm not sure. I have been so focused on helping the team, the organization, and you be successful, I probably really have not been thinking about my own future enough."

"You should. And, you should think about Sam's, too. I think she would like being so close to her grandparents."

"You're right." Charles paused. "I will l do it—on one condition."

"What's that?"

"I have to find a small farm in the vicinity. We're getting a pony, you know!"

"Yes, I heard. I'll send you the name of a real estate guy who I'm sure can find you a farm. Are you available this weekend to start looking?"

"Are you pushing me?"

"Yes. Yes, I am," Blake laughed. "There's one more thing I want to say."

"And that is?"

"I figured out why you've been successful here and throughout your career."

"Why?" Charles asked.

"Because you understand leaders who want to be great must be willing to serve."

Epilogue

Charles found a farm and bought Sam a pony. He and Sam both loved living near his parents. His recovery is ongoing, and he now talks of years sober, not days.

The team's plan was adopted. Most of the senior leaders in the organization got on board quickly. Some, more slowly, and a few were unable to embrace the change. Blake made hard decisions and released those leaders who could not change. Once a strategy is established, even senior leaders don't have the option to opt out.

The team grew stronger, too—as individuals and in number. The goal was to accelerate the plan the team had created. Gary, Kim, and Rose continue today to serve in various capacities throughout the organization.

After the leadership culture became established, the notoriety created opportunities inside and outside the company. Charles's assessment of Bob's potential was realized by others as well. He was hired to be the chief learning officer at a large multinational organization.

Blake had been brought in to turn a struggling company around. He had a hunch—he believed at least part of the answer could be found in the way they thought about leadership. He was correct. A culture of heroic leaders may work for a while, but he understood the limitations of this approach. Blake's commitment to creating a leadership culture led the organization to embrace the team's strategy; as a result, they were able to take the first step to becoming a high performance organization.

Now, Blake knew the organization had a never-ending supply of its most critical asset: leaders. They were ready to create their own future. They could now say with full confidence: Leaders Made Here!

Acknowledgments

This book is the product of a search, or perhaps better described as a quest, to help leaders and organizations excel with the never-ending challenge of creating a strong leadership bench. I am grateful to have had the chance to search the planet for the best practices you just read about in this simple story.

I am also thankful for the scores of organizations that have opened their doors for me and my team over the years. Without the generosity of countless leaders whose stories have been amalgamated here, this book would not exist. This is their story. Thank you!

As with all my books, my wife Donna should receive the lion's share of praise for the readability of this manuscript. My friend Randy Gravitt was also a tremendous sounding board and editor as we approached the final draft. The editorial staff at Berrett-Koehler was insightful as usual, with special thanks to Steve Piersanti, Janice Rutledge, Sara Jane Hope, and Ken Fracaro. Thanks to Lasell Whipple, Lindsay Miller, Michael Crowley, Peter Hobbs, and Michael Bass for their design efforts. Truth, clarity, and simplicity are often illusive—thanks to all of you who helped make the lessons of this book accessible to everyone!

About the Author

Mark Miller is a business leader, best-selling author, and communicator.

Mark began writing over fifteen years ago when he teamed up with Ken Blanchard, coauthor of *The One Minute Manager,* to write *The Secret: What Great Leaders Know and Do.* Today, over 600,000 copies of *The Secret* are in print, and it has been translated into more than twenty-five languages. Mark also wrote *The Secret of Teams*, which outlines key lessons learned from a twenty-year exploration of the question "Why do some teams outperform the rest?" Next in the series was *The Heart of Leadership,* which explores how to become the type of leader people want to follow. His most recent book, *Chess Not Checkers*, released in April 2015, is a blueprint for helping organizations reach their full potential.

In addition to his writing, Mark enjoys speaking to leaders. Over the years, he's traveled extensively around the world teaching for numerous international organizations. His theme is always the same: encouraging and equipping leaders! His topics include leadership, creativity, team building, and more.

Mark started his Chick-fil-A career working as an hourly team member in 1977. In 1978, he joined the corporate staff working in the warehouse and mailroom. Since that time, he has provided leadership for Corporate Communications, Field Operations, Quality and Customer Satisfaction, Training and Development, and Leadership Development. During his tenure with Chick-fil-A, the company has grown from seventy-five restaurants to over two thousand locations in forty-six states and the District of Columbia with annual sales approaching $8 billion.

Mark lives an active lifestyle. As a photographer, he has enjoyed shooting in some of the world's hardest-to-reach places, including Antarctica, Everest Base Camp, the jungles of Rwanda, and the Galápagos Islands.

Married to Donna, his high school sweetheart, for over thirty years, Mark has two sons, Justin and David, a daughter-in-love, Lindsay, and one amazing granddaughter, Addie!

Mark would love to connect with you via . . .

Cell: **678-612-8441**
Twitter: **@LeadersServe**
LinkedIn: **Mark Miller**

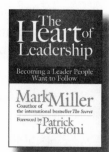
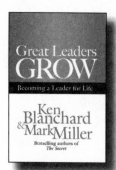

Berrett–Koehler
Publishers

Berrett-Koehler is an independent publisher dedicated to an ambitious mission: *Connecting people and ideas to create a world that works for all.*

We believe that the solutions to the world's problems will come from all of us, working at all levels: in our organizations, in our society, and in our own lives. Our BK Business books help people make their organizations more humane, democratic, diverse, and effective (we don't think there's any contradiction there). Our BK Currents books offer pathways to creating a more just, equitable, and sustainable society. Our BK Life books help people create positive change in their lives and align their personal practices with their aspirations for a better world.

All of our books are designed to bring people seeking positive change together around the ideas that empower them to see and shape the world in a new way.

And we strive to practice what we preach. At the core of our approach is Stewardship, a deep sense of responsibility to administer the company for the benefit of all of our stakeholder groups including authors, customers, employees, investors, service providers, and the communities and environment around us. Everything we do is built around this and our other key values of quality, partnership, inclusion, and sustainability.

This is why we are both a B-Corporation and a California Benefit Corporation—a certification and a for-profit legal status that require us to adhere to the highest standards for corporate, social, and environmental performance.

We are grateful to our readers, authors, and other friends of the company who consider themselves to be part of the BK Community. We hope that you, too, will join us in our mission.

A BK Business Book

We hope you enjoy this BK Business book. BK Business books pioneer new leadership and management practices and socially responsible approaches to business. They are designed to provide you with groundbreaking and practical tools to transform your work and organizations while upholding the triple bottom line of people, planet, and profits. High-five!

To find out more, visit **www.bkconnection.com**.

Berrett–Koehler
Publishers

Connecting people and ideas
to create a world that works for all

Dear Reader,

Thank you for picking up this book and joining our worldwide community of Berrett-Koehler readers. We share ideas that bring positive change into people's lives, organizations, and society.

To welcome you, we'd like to offer you a free e-book. You can pick from among twelve of our bestselling books by entering the promotional code BKP92E here: http://www.bkconnection.com/welcome.

When you claim your free e-book, we'll also send you a copy of our e-newsletter, the *BK Communiqué*. Although you're free to unsubscribe, there are many benefits to sticking around. In every issue of our newsletter you'll find

- A free e-book
- Tips from famous authors
- Discounts on spotlight titles
- Hilarious insider publishing news
- A chance to win a prize for answering a riddle

Best of all, our readers tell us, "Your newsletter is the only one I actually read." So claim your gift today, and please stay in touch!

Sincerely,

Charlotte Ashlock
Steward of the BK Website

Questions? Comments? Contact me at bkcommunity@bkpub.com.

MIX
Paper from
responsible sources
FSC® C011935

Certified

Corporation
bcorporation.net